Forgie —
The Story of Pennwood Forge Mill

By the same author
NELLY, THE NAUGHTY DONKEY
A Quartilles Publication

FORGIE—
The Story of Pennwood Forge Mill

SUE CLARKE

Quartilles International Limited
Coggeshall, Essex

Printed and bound in Great Britain by
KNAPP DREWETT & SONS LTD.
Kingston upon Thames, Surrey
For Quartilles International Limited
30 West Street, Coggeshall, Colchester, Essex CO6 1NS

This book is set in 11/12 Baskerville

ISBN 0 903021 12 9

To "Forgie"
   For all the hours of pleasure he
   has given to millions of show
   jumping fans

ACKNOWLEDGEMENTS

Acknowledgements are due to many people for helping to make this book possible but in particular I would like to mention the following:

The Hartill family

The British Show Jumping Association

Geoff Glazzard

Paddy McMahon

Peter Robeson

Graham Terry

Sally Warren

Dorian Williams, O.B.E.

John Wrathall

CONTENTS

PHOTOGRAPHS

(Between pages 52 and 53)

FOREWORD

It is to me both a privilege and pleasure that I was asked to write the foreword to a book about the remarkable Pennwood Forge Mill.

Total honesty and rare ability are qualities seldom, if ever, found in the world today — but they come together in this show jumper to an unusual degree. There have occurred two revolutions which have transformed show jumping since the war. The first witnesses its emergence as a national sport peopled with international heroes, bringing consistent success in the major championships. Then came the era of sponsorship, together with the broadening of the base of our international teams and the development of the scene as we know it today. Forgie in his own unique way is the personification of both these phases of growth. With his uncanny sense of a special occasion and a heart second to none he represents all that is best in our sport. Moreover, there is little doubt that his many achievements were due in no small measure to his owner Fred Hartill and family in managing Forgie so well by giving him the stability and understanding he needed at all the crossroads of his career.

Furthermore, he is timeless — one does not compare him with others precisely because of that — and, because he is above ordinary yardsticks, he bears, truly the hallmark of greatness.

PETER ROBESON

1

1

MOMENTS TO REMEMBER

The crowd clap wildly as the brown horse enters the arena and looks calmly round. It's Pennwood Forge Mill, the horse who needs no introduction, the darling of the public. No blue-blooded thoroughbred this but a rather common-looking horse with a Roman nose. Maybe it is this which has made him so popular and caught the imagination of show jumping fans all over the country. The horse bought in Ireland by Fred Hartill for a mere £130 and transformed into one of the greatest show jumpers of all time. Certainly one of the most genuine and consistent and one of the biggest money spinners. Until the end of the 1978 season he had won nearly £55,000 since he started jumping 11 years previously.

Forgie is of unknown breeding although many people have claimed to own his mother, brothers and sisters! When he won the Irish Horse Board's award in 1973 they tried to trace his background but to no avail. I should think it is quite likely he has some Irish draught blood in him by his build. Although he stands 16 h.h. he is very deep through the girth with short strong legs and this gives the misleading

3

impression that he's a small stocky horse rather than a big one. His only white markings are a star and snip on his face and socks on both hand-legs.

Pennwood Forge Mill has been at the very top of the show jumping tree for eight years and done a great deal during that time. This is a long period in the life of a show jumper in these days when the big courses encountered take their toll on horses. There have been many good horses which have stayed at the top for three or four seasons but few have remained there as long or done as much as Pennwood Forge Mill. Even at the 1978 Olympia Show, Forgie, at the age of 14, showed he was still good enough to qualify for the jump-off in a couple of the big competitions. However, the strain of jumping big fences in a confined space was perhaps beginning to tell, for in the jump-offs he always seemed to lack sparkle and have two or three fences down.

I had been a fan of Forge Mill even before I came to live in Warwickshire for there is something about the horse which makes you love him. I can well remember the first time I saw him jump. It was at Harwood Hall in 1971 when he and Beau Supreme fought out the finish of the Puissance. As my car has travelled the well-worn route to Pennwood, I've come to learn more about Forgie and discover his likes and dislikes from his present groom Valerie Hartill and Sally Warren who used to look after him. For instance, he loves 'Polos', ice creams and chocolates but hates being clipped and also shows a dislike of camels.

Paddy McMahon's name is the one which will be best associated with Pennwood Forge Mill, for together they built up a great partnership and went right to the top of the show jumping ladder. In 1973 they brought off a unique treble by winning the European Show Jumping Championship at Hickstead, the Horse and Hound Cup and the King George V Gold Cup, all in six short days. Few who were privileged to see it will forget their classic round to win the Ronson Trophy on the final night of the 1972 Horse of the Year Show. They helped us to win many Nations Cups, always being relied on to jump a good dependable round and very often pulling off a double clear. When I asked Ronnie Masserella, team manager, for a quote about Pennwood Forge Mill he replied, "I don't know what to say. What can you say about him? He's been such a marvellous horse and it was always a privilege to have him on a team. He always gave of his best and helped us to many Nations Cup victories".

When I asked Paddy McMahon which win had given him the most pleasure, he thought for a few seconds (for there have been so many) before replying, "The King George V Gold Cup because it's the competition everybody wants to win". It was also a marvellous moment for him to meet the Queen who said to Paddy and Fred Hartill, "You must be very proud of Pennwood Forge Mill". This win came just **three days after he had clinched the 1973 European Show** Jumping title after a gruelling three days at Hickstead and two days after he'd won the Horse and Hound Cup on the opening night of the Royal International Horse Show.

Another win which sticks in Paddy's mind is, of course, the 1972 Ronson Trophy at the Horse of the Year Show. Dorian Williams in his book "Great Moments in Sport: Show Jumping" describes it far better than I ever could and has kindly given permission to re-print it here:

"But it was on the last night of all that the crowd really rose to a British victory. In the final event — a two-round competition for the Victor Ludorum of the whole show — there were eventually four British riders, three German riders and young Eddie Macken from Ireland, showing such remarkable promise in his first international show, left in with a chance. These were the riders who, out of twenty-five starters, had achieved double clear rounds.

Simona, ridden by Steenken for Germany, went first and had a clear round. From then onwards, over this very demanding course being jumped against the clock, there were no clear rounds until the third German rider, Paul

Schockemöhle (the brother of the more famous Alwin) riding Abadir, came in and managed to beat Steenken's time by a full two seconds. This really did seem to be absolutely invincible.

Pennwood Forge Mill entered the arena. Paddy McMahon looked anxious as he rode him round waiting for the bell, and it seemed as though the crowd, too, were anxious to show their appreciation of the fact that Britain was still in with a chance. Defeat seemed probable, yet many in the audience who had either been there in person or had watched it on television had not forgotten Forge Mill's great performance in the Puissance two nights earlier, or his magnificent effort in the Hickstead Jumping Derby when he may well have been unlucky not to have won, or the effortless way in which he dominated the Olympic trial at British Timken. But surely, against the clock, in a small indoor arena, this was not Forge Mill's metier at all.

Yet, somehow, that vast, tense crowd sensed that Paddy McMahon and Forge Mill were determined to win. I have never heard on any other occasion a cheer start as a horse approached the first fence. It was as though the moment the bell had gone and the last British horse had started the pent-up emotions had been released. It was as though the crowd hoped that Forge Mill could be borne on the wings of a cheer — and so it was. As he rose at the first fence, the cheer started. It increased in a steady crescendo as he went round the course of eight fences. As he turned for the last two and the crowd somehow found themselves able to snatch a glance at the great electric clock hanging over the centre of the arena, they realised that Forge Mill could, in fact, beat Abadir's time, and so this tremendous cheer rose now to a vast shout — of ecstasy, excitement, hope and anticipation.

Unbelievably it all worked. I do indeed believe that Forge Mill and Paddy McMahon were inspired by that tremendous cheer, finding somehow a reserve of strength previously unknown to them and, more important, a reserve of speed. As Pennwood Forge Mill flashed through the finish the clock stopped and then ten thousand pairs of eyes turned to it. Twenty-eight point three; Forge Mill had won the Ronson Trophy from the might of Germany by just ·1 of a second.

It was not the rider this time who threw his cap into the air as he left the ring; rather it was the spectators, who threw anything and everything that they could lay hands on in the air. Seldom, if ever, have I witnessed such a scene of rejoicing.

Certainly Pennwood Forge Mill and Paddy McMahon were the heroes of the hour, and they returned to a tremendous reception when they came in to receive the trophy; a reception repeated a few minutes later when they took their place in the great cavalcade that bring the Horse of the Year Show to an end."

Afterwards when walking in the street strangers would stop Paddy and talk to him about his victory — he was a national hero. Perhaps this fine win helped to make up for the disappointment of being left out of our Munich Olympic team. This talented rider had been very anxious to get selected and this had come through in his riding, making him too desperate, especially at combination fences which he knew were Forge Mill's weakness.

On Forgie's first trip abroad to Ostend in 1971 he covered himself in glory by winning the Grand Prix, a proud moment for all those associated with him as the Union Jack was raised and the National Anthem rang out across the arena. He was to go on to represent his country on 32 occasions and helped to win seven Nations Cups. Since H.R.H. Prince Philip presented the President's Trophy in 1965 it has come to Great Britain on eight occasions with Forge Mill contributing to our success in 1972, 1973, 1974, 1977 and 1978.

Paddy took over the ride in 1971 but it was Graham Terry who first sat on him when he arrived from Ireland with a reputation for being a 'rogue' horse, difficult to ride. He then went to Northamptonshire farmer John Wrathall for three seasons and John, with endless patience and under-standing, brought him from a novice to Grade A and took him to the Horse of the Year Show in 1970. When Paddy and Fred Hartill parted company at the beginning of 1977 the success story continued with Geoff Glazzard, the virtually unknown rider from Wolverhampton, who accepted the great challenge offered him and took on and beat the best.

For Geoff, his greatest moments have been his equal first with David Broome in the Butlins Championship at the 1977 Horse of the Year Show and his victory in the Horse and Hound Cup at the Royal International Horse Show in July of 1978. Both Paddy and Geoff agree that Forgie will always try his hardest, for he's so honest.

At the end of each season the British Show Jumping Association publish a list of the Top Twenty Money Winning Horses, National, International and Combined, and since 1972 Pennwood Forge Mill's name has never been missing. He headed all three tables in 1972, the Combined list in 1973 and was third Internationally and seventh in the National chart. During the year of the World Champion-ships, 1974, he slipped to eighth in the National, sixth International and fifth Combined. In 1975 he was fourth National, sixth International and fourth Combined; 1976, however, saw him back at the top of the National tree and sixth in the Combined totals. In his first season with Geoff Glazzard (1977) he finished third in the National table, was sixteenth Internationally and eighth in the Combined list. During 1978 he finished tenth in the National table, twelfth in the International and eleventh in the Combined. Proof of his consistency, if any is indeed needed.

He has won no less than 16 Area International Trials up until the end of the 1978 season and has been placed in 34 others. It is a wonderful record over these big courses and he is rarely out of the money. His wins included three during his first season with Paddy McMahon, at Staffordshire County, Hull and Bakewell, three in 1977 with Geoff

Glazzard, and two last season, at Anglesey and Vauxhall Motors.

The Olympic (now called International) Trial at British Timken is a competition in which he has always done well, winning in 1972 and 1977 and being second in 1974. Forgie loves the Royal Show at Stoneleigh and has a good record there. He has won the Texaco Trophy on three occasions, in 1972, 1973 and 1976, and was third in 1975, the year he won the Hennessey Trophy. He was second in the Supreme Championship in 1973 (when he got caught up in the timing wires) and again in 1977, and fourth in 1978.

During the peak of his career Pennwood Forge Mill was very versatile, just as capable of winning a puissance as a speed class or Grand Prix. He could adapt to the different competitions without trouble and found coming indoors to Wembley for the Royal International no problem after the vast open spaces of Hickstead and this was proved by his treble in 1973. Forge Mill loves his jumping and rises to the crowd. He always jumps better at shows where there are lots of spectators, for he adores people. However, he's not so keen on other horses, although he loves small ponies, like his faithful companion Magpie, and donkeys. The one exception was the late Hartwig Steenken's Simona whom he clearly adored — and she was quite keen on him too!

Fred Hartill's history is steeped in horses and ponies for his father dealt in horses besides having butchers' shops in Sedgley. One thing which makes Fred Hartill very sad is that his father, a great horseman in his day, did not live to see Forge Mill achieve greatness, for he would have been so proud of him.

Pennwood Forge Mill lives at Penn on the outskirts of industrial Wolverhampton. Set high on a hill from Mount Farm you can see the lights of Sedgley and Wolverhampton on two sides. But looking ahead, Penn Golf Club runs up to a village with the attractive name of Gospel End Village, whilst in a south-westerly direction the Clee Hills stretch for miles towards Hereford. Penn Common itself covers some

147 acres.

The origin of how Pennwood Forge Mill came to be named is interesting. One evening, Fred Hartill's old friend of many years standing, Jack Skidmore, was sitting chatting when Valerie Hartill came into the room to say that they must choose names for a couple of horses which were jumping the following day. They decided to call one Stonehaven and Fred said, "Why don't we name the other one after your farm?" so he was duly called Pennwood Forge Mill. Little did they realise what a great horse he was to become, but it is fitting that he should be named after the farm of a great show jumping enthusiast such as Jack Skidmore. He proudly describes himself as Black Country born and bred and still farms at Forge Mill Farm, West Bromwich. He has been associated with show jumping for 55 years and although not taking an active part since 1950 still enjoys helping others.

Before the war Jack used to jump one of the best animals around at the time. Called Aircraft she only stood 14.1½h.h. but could take on and beat the best in the country. It was from Jack that Fred Hartill bought his first show jumper after the war. She was called Bay Bibi (Indian for woman) and Jack was pleased to get rid of her for £50 as she had a big buck and he couldn't stand her. But fortunately she and Fred hit it off and they won seven firsts from seven shows during the August Bank Holiday week.

I asked Jack Skidmore if he could remember Forge Mill jumping in the early days. He didn't see him very much at the start but remembers that one evening he received a phone call from Fred Hartill asking him to watch out for Forge Mill the following day at the City of Birmingham Show. This he did and reported back with the following comment, "I think he's a useful horse". He now considers Forge Mill the best horse we've seen show jumping since the war, even greater than Foxhunter.

Everybody makes a fuss of Forge Mill. He is so intelligent and held in great esteem by all. He's full of character, with the instincts of a thoroughbred horse, being so quick thinking. We will be fortunate if we ever see another horse which achieves as much as Pennwood Forge Mill has over the past 11 years.

2

LIFE IN IRELAND

Forgie's breeding is shrouded in mystery but, thanks to the help of a number of people in Ireland, I have been able to discover some of his past history. Fred Hartill told me, "A lot of people have offered me his mother, brothers and sisters, but the truth of the matter is we don't know his breeding". This reminds me of the lovely story of the English buyer going to look at young horses in an Irish dealer's yard and, on asking what one was by, the dealer replied, "Well, now, what would you like it to be by?".

It has since been established that Forgie was sent to Ballina Foal Fair in County Mayo, where he was bought by the late James Crossan who lived in the south of Ireland. Crossan knew that John McCaughey from the North was looking for some foals so he gave him a ring and told him to come over and look at some he'd just bought. John duly hitched up his trailer and came to have a look. He selected three, including a brown gelding with a rather common head, and set off back home. At the border post the guard asked him what he had in the trailer, to which he replied, "Three foals". "Well", said the guard, "you must have lost

13

one, for there are only two here now". On retracing his steps it transpired that the third, Forge Mill, had jumped out over the end of the trailer some six miles back. To this day he still bears the scar on his shoulder sustained in his leap and Fred Hartill feels that this incident had much to do with the delinquent behaviour of his youth.

McCaughey sent him to Banbridge Sales as a youngster where he was bought by W. J. (Billy) Sinton who lives at Scarva just outside Belfast. On arriving back from the sales there was a man in the yard looking for a young hunter. His name, by coincidence, was also Sinton, although Tim is no relation. When he saw the horse coming down the ramp he took a fancy to him and bought him for £120.

This was in the spring of 1967 and Tim Sinton decided to call him Duster for there was a story (which has not been proved) that he was by Blue Duster. He started to break him and got him going well on the lunge. Being rather busy he asked his friends Jimmy and Elize Cockburn who live about eight miles away if they would break the horse for him. Although normally they only break their own horses they agreed to help Tim out and Duster was duly despatched to them. They lunged him and found that he seemed to know a lot for a horse which was reputably unbroken.

Then came the day for Jimmy to get on him in the stable, with Elize at his head. All went smoothly, as it did when they mounted him in the yard and, eventually, in the field. One day Jimmy was late back from work so Elize decided she would ride Duster by herself for he had been so good. She stayed on for only 20 seconds or so for he bucked and bucked and then, on reaching the hedge at the side of the field, stood up on his hind legs and came over backwards. Fortunately he just missed Elize, who had thrown herself clear, but he kicked her several times on the bottom as he struggled to get up. Elize and Jimmy are convinced that he had been ridden before and knew just how to get rid of his rider. They tried restricting him so that he didn't have the freedom to buck, but still he managed it, so there was nothing for it but to send the horse back to Tim Sinton, for Elize had young twins of three and didn't want to get herself injured. He, in turn, returned him to Billy Sinton.

Despite the way he treated her, Elize remembers him as an essentially kind horse with lots of character, and their children could do anything with him in the stable. Jimmy Cockburn is a Joint-Master of the County Down Staghounds and Elize is treasurer and they, like Tim Sinton, are keen hunting people. They are delighted that Forge Mill has gone on to do so well, for if they had kept him he'd never have been discovered.

The horse was turned out for the summer at Billy Sinton's farm and it was here that Fred Hartill found him. He had been to Kilrush Fair in County Clare with Harold Lusk, the Northern dealer and brother of well-known trainer, Brian, and had bid for and purchased a number of horses. During the course of the day they met Billy Sinton who told them he had some nice young horses for sale. They called in at his yard on the way home the following day to take a look for themselves as Fred Hartill still had some space left in his box. Billy asked him if he'd like to buy one which he admitted was bad to ride, so Fred paid £130 for the horse which was to become one of the greatest show jumpers of all time — Pennwood Forge Mill.

Hundreds of other Pennwood horses have been bought from the dealers around Belfast, but although there have been a lot of good ones there's never been another Forge Mill. "When you have the intelligence, the ability, the natural big jump, it's very easy to hurry a horse", Fred Hartill recollects. "It was perhaps fortunate that he was difficult because it made us put more time into him and not rush him."

The Cockburns heard that Forge Mill had been sold to a Mr. Fred Hartill and often wondered how he was getting on with the horse and whether he was experiencing the same difficulties they had. Just what sort of problems they encountered at Pennwood will be made clear as you read on.

15

What is certain is that the long hours of driving him in long reins paid dividends because now, when he goes against the clock, he can turn so quickly on landing over a fence. It makes them supple and obedient and they are always going forward. I personally feel it is a great pity that the art of long reining seems for many people breaking horses to be a thing of the past.

The next time the Cockburns and Tim Sinton heard of the horse was when they received a phone call from Billy Sinton telling them that 'their' horse was on television, jumping at the Royal International Horse Show. They quickly turned on to find Duster, as they knew him, competing with the cream of the show jumpers. He had come a long way.

Fred Hartill used to buy the majority of his horses in Ireland for he feels they make the best jumpers, due to the fact they've mostly been driven in harness and are therefore less inclined to nappiness than a horse which has only been lunged. However, the prices are so high over there nowadays, with inflation and the vast sums paid by Continental buyers, that he now purchases less and less from that source.

The collecting ring area at Ballsbridge, scene of the famous Dublin Horse Show each August, is known as the pocket. One day Fred Hartill and Paddy McMahon were standing here waiting for the all-clear for Paddy to walk the course. A chap came up to them and started chatting and when Paddy had gone into the ring he bought Fred a drink in the bar and said to him, "I know Fred Hartill very well and in fact found him Forge Mill". Fred didn't say anything but when he'd finished his drink he handed the man a business card and said, "Let me know if you find another one like him!".

3

EARLY DAYS AT PENNWOOD

When Forgie arrived at Pennwood in the autumn of 1967 as a three-year-old he proved very difficult. It took months of patience and understanding to make him rideable so that he could be taken out for a quiet hack around the countryside and walk, trot and canter around the school without bucking his rider off — at least not too often!

The yard at Mount Farm consists of some 30 boxes and a complex of old-fashioned-type stalls with chains behind them. It was in one of these that Forgie was put when unloaded from Ireland. Lesson number one was to be able to tie him up without him running back. This was gradually accomplished and for a few days the girl grooms just talked to him and groomed him to gain his trust and confidence. He was given time to settle in before anybody attempted to mount him.

Graham Terry was the man who had the dubious pleasure of being the first person to ride him at Pennwood. Graham has a long association with the Hartill family since the age of eight and was chosen because of his experience over the years of breaking and schooling many different Pennwood horses and ponies.

Graham first met Fred Hartill some 32 years ago when, as an eight-year-old schoolboy, he spent every possible spare moment at the forge of Wolverhampton blacksmith, Mr. Norton. Being horse mad he would cycle from his home to watch the skilled man at work. At first he stood by the door, not daring to go any nearer, but gradually he was bold enough to edge a little closer on each visit. The blacksmith would tell him to go away but he was a determined little chap and in the end Mr. Norton gave him the job of oiling the horses' feet when he had finished shoeing them. Graham was very proud of his job.

It was in this setting that Fred Hartill found him when taking some horses from the riding school in Sedgley Bullring to be shod there. The journey was three miles and they would ride one and lead three or four others, often going back on the bus for another batch whilst the first was being done. Not then the luxury of the travelling blacksmith or a lorry to take them to the forge.

Describing the meeting, Fred Hartill told me, "There was the loveliest little black-haired fellow there and the blacksmith asked me if I could find a job for him as he was horse mad". Fred had a big 16.3 h.h. mare called Socks who had cost £24 when in a very poor condition at an auction. This was in 1937 when the going rate for a pair of pony shoes was ten shillings and twelve shillings and sixpence for hunters. Fred Hartill told Graham that if he could get up on Socks by the time he'd counted to ten he'd give him a job at the stables. Graham was not going to miss a chance like this and somehow clambered up on to the big horse, saying, with an eager grin, "Well, have I got the job then?".

He duly turned up the following Saturday with his haversack and the new anorak his mother had bought him in honour of the occasion. His first day at the stables didn't go exactly smoothly. First job was to go to the field to catch the horses, ready for the riding lessons. As they all gathered round the corn bucket one horse picked Graham up by his new anorak and shook him. But he was not easily daunted and led the horse into the yard. In his inexperience he made the mistake of tying it to the back of a cart in the yard where new stables were under construction. When some buckets were banged together the horse panicked and drew back, dragging the cart with it. He backed into a wall, sitting down on it, before somebody could untie the frightened animal.

Not a very auspicious start. Everything seemed to be going wrong for Graham that first day but he didn't get the sack. As he went to go home, Mr. Hartill asked him how he'd enjoyed his first day. "I was scared to death all day, it was smashing!" replied Graham. So, as Fred Hartill told me jokingly, he was installed and they couldn't get rid of him! At first Graham only came on Saturdays, although he was longing to come on Sundays, too, but hadn't been asked. So on a Sunday he used to cycle to Sedgley from Wolverhampton and watch the rides at Millbank from behind a tree. Then came the big day when he was invited to come on a Sunday and this thrilled him.

He was christened 'Sparkey' after a pony which he was very fond of and which had been sold on. By riding all the various ponies Graham soon became a competent rider and developed a natural seat. He and another young rider, Mary Draisey, were installed as chief breakers for the small ponies which Fred Hartill and his brother Bill were too big to ride. This was in the days when rodeos were popular and Graham was star performer at all the local ones. He would often accompany the Hartills to shows, in due course jumping some of the ponies in the ring himself. At this time Fred Hartill was doing a lot of jumping, his best-known horse being Pennwood Gold Flake on which he won many awards.

Against the advice of Fred Hartill, at the age of 15 Graham went into racing but soon became disenchanted with it. Mr. Hartill suggested that he learnt a trade not connected with horses, just treating show jumping as a hobby. So he arranged for him to go into one of his father's butchers' shops in Sedgley. On one occasion they were busy working in the shop when Fred Hartill said, "I've got eight horses to take to the show tomorrow. You can ride two if you get finished early in the shop". So overjoyed was Graham that he forgot to concentrate on what he was doing, knocked Fred's arm and Fred chopped off the end of his finger instead of the meat! The irony of the story is that Graham got the ride on six horses and Fred Hartill rode two with one hand—so perhaps it wasn't an accident!

For five years Graham stuck to butchering but then decided to go into the printing trade. He now runs his own company in Harborne, Birmingham; living at Shirley with his wife, Sandra, and their young son. There are usually two or three horses around and a pony, and even though he's now moved away from the area he regularly calls in at Pennwood for a chat and to reminisce about old times.

But to get back to the story of Pennwood Forge Mill . . . When Forgie was given a feed Graham would hold on to the beam above his stall and gently lower himself on to his back. In the security of his own stall Forgie didn't attempt anything naughty and learnt to accept the weight on his back, but it was a long time before he would accept a surcingle or girth around him. He was therefore lunged on just a head-collar at first but eventually it was possible to drive him in long reins around the school and later along the lanes surrounding Penn Common.

One day when Graham was driving him around the indoor school a horse became loose in the yard and galloped out, making a terrible din. Fred Hartill, hearing the commotion, rushed up to the school to tear a strip off whoever had let the horse go. He burst into the school just as Forgie was going past, frightening him so that he shied. Graham lost the reins and the horse galloped loose around the school, going into orbit over the practice fence. This was a fateful day for it was then that Fred Hartill and Graham realised what a potentially good horse they had, for he could really leap. So excited were they that Fred forgot to go and see what had happened to the loose horse! Pennwood Gold Flake was brought out of her stable to act as a lead horse for Forgie and he followed her, really jumping well. Fred Hartill said to Graham, "If it takes two years to school him then we've got to do it".

It was fortunate for the Hartills and all those associated with Forgie that he was rather a wayward character. Otherwise, he would, like all Pennwood horses, have been sold because it is a dealing yard. He was so wild during those first weeks that he couldn't be shown to prospective buyers although he was then valued in the Pennwood books at £250. Graham well remembers his first ride on Forgie when he was loose, although he had sat up on him first in the stall and then on the lunge. They managed one circuit of the indoor school with the rider hitting the deck on no fewer than five occasions, so big was his buck. But this cheerful character was not deterred by all the bangs and bruises and persevered. It was a long struggle but eventually Graham felt he was getting somewhere. The horse was going quite nicely on either rein at the walk, trot and canter.

In those days Pennwood was run as a riding school and Graham and Forgie would often tag on to the end of a ride given by Mr. Tate, the chief instructor. Graham considers this an excellent way of getting a young horse going. For they follow the example of experienced horses, and it releases some of the pressure from the rider as he doesn't have to think about pushing the horse forward the whole time and can concentrate on other things.

Fred Hartill is a firm believer in teaching youngsters to jump by this method. The first time a young horse jumps a set of coloured fences he sends him round behind a school-master. "They see the older horse doing it and follow suit and eventually you get it into their computer that when there's a fence there they have to jump it. If in the early days you begin to school a youngster over coloured poles and he stops, he establishes that he's able to, and you've got problems — you're teaching him bad habits."

21

One day Graham was asked by Fred Hartill how Forgie was going. On hearing that all was well he said he'd like to see him in the indoor school that evening for a demonstration. When Mr. and Mrs. Hartill arrived, Graham walked the horse around the school, broke into a trot, and still Forgie behaved impeccably. He urged him into a canter, they reached the top end of the school and, wham!, there was Graham being catapulted up into the rafters. Luckily he came back down in the saddle, only for Forgie to give another gigantic buck which put him on the floor — and in front of the boss, too! All the long hours of hard work gone in a few seconds.

It was decided to turn the horse out for a while and then have another go. They found that although he could be hacked around the lanes and ridden around the school, he could regularly put in an enormous buck which landed Graham on the deck. It never paid to be complacent with him because if you squeezed a little too hard with your legs he would have you off as quick as a flash. Despite his bad habits they had a lot of fun with the horse for he was a great character, a loveable rogue. He adored his jumping and when faced with a small obstacle would buck and squeal his way down to it, jump it like a stag and buck going away from it. It was a matter of time and patience to resolve his problems.

4

JOHN WRATHALL'S TRAINING

When the time came for Forge. Mill to start his jumping career it was decided to send him to John Wrathall who had been a business associate of Fred Hartill's for some years. John farms at Welford in Northamptonshire and is a wizard at producing young horses, always having a few about the place. He told me that when the horse came to him in the back end of 1967 he was still very frightened of your legs and his theory is that the horse had, at some time, run away with somebody. For the first five minutes after you mounted him you could only walk. John, too, found the horse had a big buck and was dropped on a few occasions, including once at a show when Forgie bucked him off after the practice fence.

With endless patience John brought the big horse on slowly, upgrading him to 'A', and took him to the Horse of the Year Show. Fred Hartill is full of praise for the way John moulded his career, and is very much aware what a debt he and the show-jumping public owe to him for not hurrying the horse and spoiling him. Far too many horses are spoilt nowadays by being rushed against the clock before they are ready for it. There were times when John would take him to a show but if he didn't like the course or the going was bad he would box him up again and take him home without jumping him. These cautious days paid off for they meant the horse was never hurried or rushed before his time. I asked John if he could remember the first show and he told me it was at Pitsford where, if his memory serves him rightly, the horse had one fence down.

Their first season together was in 1968 as a four-year-old, when he was placed in 16 classes winning £49 but not a red rosette. Forgie's first rosette came in the Foxhunter Competition at the Staffordshire County Show on 2nd June 1968 when he finished second. Jeremy Houghton-Brown, B.S.J.A. course builder and judge and former Centre Manager at the National Equestrian Centre, Stoneleigh, well remembers the hard work and skill put in by John Wrathall. He told me that he first saw Pennwood Forge Mill jumping at Burley-on-the-Hill Show when he was very taken with the horse, who jumped a superb clear round, apart from missing a fence. The commentator announced a clear round so John Wrathall had to be honest and go and confess to the judges that he'd forgotten to jump one fence! So much did Jeremy like the horse that he sent some Greek buyers to see him but they couldn't (fortunately for the sake of British show jumping) raise the money so he stayed with John.

The following season he had his first taste of the wide open spaces of the All England Jumping Course at Hickstead where some years later he was to win the European Show Jumping title with Paddy McMahon. He took three minor placings in Grade 'C' competitions. On 27th May 1969 came the big day when he won his first red rosette when landing the Grade 'C' class at Wollaston Show. I asked John Wrathall if he realised then what a brilliant horse he had in his care and he told me that right from the start he thought he was brilliant. He was 100% genuine and he felt he had a lot of ability. He, too, found him a kind horse with no vices at all in the stable. By the middle of June Forgie had reached Grade 'B', having won £100. He and John went on to win the Open at East Leake Show about a month later, also the Grades 'B' and 'C' classes at Northampton County, but it was at Alwalton that they took their first major class, the East of England Grade 'B' Championship. On 9th August he became a Grade 'A' show jumper, having won £200, and he ended the season well by finishing second in the Adult Championship at the City of Birmingham Show.

At the end of the 1969 season the B.S.J.A. decided to revise the gradings and a horse had to win £300 to be in the top grade. Forgie, with total winnings of £271 9s., therefore found himself back in Grade 'B' at the start of the 1970 season on the revised winnings. But it wasn't long before he was again in the top bracket. Once more he travelled to Sussex for the Hickstead Easter meeting, finishing third in two Popular Open competitions. These events are open only to horses which have not won a certain amount of money in the previous season, therefore debarring the better horses and giving the younger ones a chance.

Area International Trials are designed to act as a shop window for potential International horses and riders, with a big track being put up to sort the men from the boys. Forgie competed in his first A.I.T. at Leicester Show on 6th June 1970 and far from disgraced himself, finishing equal fifth. He was also equal sixth in the Cheshire A.I.T. and at Liverpool had a good show, winning the Grade 'A' class against tough opposition.

Pennwood Forge Mill joined the elite in 1970 by qualifying for the Horse of the Year Show at Wembley, the ambition of all riders. In preparation for his first big indoor show John took him to Harwood Hall in Essex, the establishment so well run by Cindy Mead, and to Park Farm for his final work-out for the electric atmosphere of the Wembley arena. John remembers that he didn't go very well at the beginning of the week but improved each day to finish a creditable sixth in the Dick Turpin Stakes and equal seventh in the Wembley Stakes.

When Fred Hartill took the horse back to Pennwood it was a very sad John who saw him go, the horse had so much ability and always gave of his best. He compares his consistency with that of Wilf White's Nizefella, who, had show jumping been as widely shown on TV as nowadays, would he feels have been as popular with the general public as Pennwood Forge Mill is today. John had done a marvellous job. He did all the spadework, being very much a horseman with perhaps not such a stong competitive streak as Forgie's later riders.

5

PADDY TAKES OVER THE REINS

Paddy McMahon is a name which sounds very Irish but his closest connection with the Emerald Isle was two generations ago when his grandparents came from Dundalk. Paddy was born in Derbyshire on 15th December 1933 and has lived in England all his life.

His background is not at all horsey for he didn't ride until he was 14 and was then completely self-taught. He went to school with Mr. Tommy Mulholland's son and for one season rode his J.A. ponies before going on to horses. On leaving school he joined the Mulholland yard, schooling and producing many young horses. Probably the best known of his mounts during his time at Derby was the grand veteran, Tim II, which he rode for ten years. He, like Forge Mill, was very popular with the crowds and during the heyday of his career the pair won the then record first prize in British show jumping of £1,000. This was put up by the News of the World at the Ascot Jumping Show which used to be run on the racecourse by Lavinia, Duchess of Norfolk, and her daughter, Lady Sarah Fitzalan-Howard, herself a keen show jumper. Paddy also took the horse on a tour of the American shows and won the 1958 B.S.J.A. National Championship. Other novices he produced and upgraded to 'A' included Mourne Lass, Sun Cottage and Echo.

From Mr. Mulholland, Paddy went to work for the Cottams, riding horses such as St. David and Warpaint, which went on to be jumped by Harvey Smith. Fred Hartill first came across Paddy one day at a show when Paddy asked him if Pennwood Gold Flake was for sale. He came to try her at Pennwood and on leaving said that if Fred ever wanted a rider for her he would be interested. Soon afterwards he rang to ask if he could jump the horse for he had heard that Fred Hartill had hurt his neck again and couldn't ride. Fred agreed to him riding Gold Flake and gradually he started jumping other Pennwood horses and a year later joined the staff.

He stayed for three years before joining Trevor Banks' Yorkshire string where he spent another three years. During this time he went abroad with the British team, riding Hideaway. What a great horse he has been, taking part in two Olympic Games, at Munich in 1972 with Mike Saywell and Montreal in 1976 with Graham Fletcher, besides giving Captain Mark Phillips a lift up the show jumping ladder.

At the beginning of 1971 Paddy approached Fred Hartill to ask if he could rejoin the Pennwood string. So it was that Forge Mill was brought back from John Wrathall and taken to the top of the show-jumping tree by Paddy McMahon, who had experience of riding international horses abroad. John Wrathall had done a fine job in bringing the horse to this level of his career, few could have done better.

It is Paddy McMahon's name which will be best associated with Pennwood Forge Mill for he rode the horse from 1971 until the end of the 1976 season, and it was during this period that Forgie had some of his greatest wins and was at the peak of his career. When Paddy took over the ride he fully realised the potential of Forge Mill before he ever sat on him, having noticed him at the Horse of the Year Show. He had Paddy on the floor more than once and he recollects, "He used to shoot you off, so powerful were his hindquarters. The first time it happened, he looked very surprised to see me on the ground and peered down at me with his big brown eyes. I couldn't be cross with him, I just had to laugh".

Paddy and Pennwood Forge Mill soon struck up a good understanding and were quickly into their stride. It was at Royal Windsor in May that people first began to sit up and take notice of the combination. They were fourth in the Radicon Stakes and St. George Stakes and fifth in the Supreme Championship. Forgie won his first Area International Trial at Staffordshire County in May, then another at Hull at the end of July, where he also walked away with the Gentlemen's Championship. The selectors were beginning to watch Paddy McMahon and Pennwood Forge Mill. A third in the Area International Trial at Bakewell and second at Anglesey Show was enough to convince them he should be selected to travel to Ostend at the end of August with the British team. They were being hailed in the Press as the stars of the future.

Although Paddy had competed abroad with Tim II and Hideaway, Forge Mill was very much the new boy on trial. He did not let the side down, covering himself in glory by winning the Grand Prix over a formidable course and against tough opposition. There were only two in the jump-off, the other being Eddie Macken. The young Irishman, going first, had a fence down and Douglas Bunn, our Chef d'Equipe, told Paddy to go in there and beat the time. But Paddy said he intended to clear the fences, too, and didn't want to rush Forge Mill against the clock. The pair went in and jumped a lovely clear to score a fine win for Britain. They also finished third in the Puissance (Test), jumping 6 ft. 10 in. The British Show Jumping Association were carrying out a policy of sending as many new caps abroad as possible and the Ostend team included three other newcomers, Johnny Kidd, Auriole Ferguson and Derek Ricketts. Aileen Ross (who later became Lady Frazer) made up the team.

After Forgie's victory in the Grand Prix there were great celebrations in the British camp that evening but the next day it was back to work for the important Nations Cup. In this Forge Mill and Paddy jumped clear first time but had eight faults in the second round, with Britain dropping to second place behind Ireland. It is interesting to note that included in the Irish team was a young man described by one reporter as "Iris Kellett's promising protégé, E. Macken, on Oatfield Hills" — how right he was!

Dougie Bunn, master of Hickstead and Chef d'Equipe at Ostend, contributes the following about Pennwood Forge Mill: —

"Pennwood Forge Mill is one of the most brilliant horses seen since the war. Much of his success is due to the fact he wasn't hurried and was taken to a lot of smaller shows before tackling the big competitions. Immediately I saw the horse I thought he was good. He's rather like the Michelin tyre man, always having a spare spring other horses seem to lack. His biggest win was probably the European Championship at Hickstead in 1973 when he proved a highly popular winner over a very testing course. He also went well in the World Championships the following year until the third leg when he got into trouble in the combination, as did a lot of other horses. To sum it up briefly, he's a winner."

This was a fine start to their International career and success was so much sweeter because it was unexpected. Pennwood Forge Mill was an outstanding young horse of great potential and he gained many admirers in Ostend. Tears of happiness were streaming down the face of his groom Sally Warren as the Union Jack was raised and the strains of the National Anthem rang out across the arena. Her great favourite Forge Mill, or Plonk as she called him, had won the first of many International competitions.

From Ostend the team travelled on to Rotterdam where again he went well to be chosen for our Nations Cup team. He was the only British horse to achieve two clears, despite a nasty moment at the water in the second round when he put in a short stride. We once more finished second, this time to Germany, the other members of our team being Harvey Smith with Mattie Brown, Alan Oliver with Sweep III and David Broome and Sportsman. This was a friendly show, with horses, owners, riders and grooms being well looked after.

Returning to England it was time to get ready for the Horse of the Year Show at the beginning of October. This used to be the grand finale of the home jumping season and indeed still is for the show horses and ponies. However, the jumpers now have various indoor shows all winter, the main one being the Olympia Show, organised by Raymond Brooks-Ward just before Christmas. The atmosphere at Wembley still retains its unique end-of-term flavour and a win there holds a great deal of prestige.

Many horses find the transition from the wide open arenas to the confined space of the 200 ft. × 80 ft. area at Wembley difficult, but Forgie has always adapted very quickly. As preparation Paddy took him to the indoor show at Harwood Hall where he won a speed class in decisive fashion. He was also second in the Puissance, fighting it out over the 6 ft. 3 in. wall with Beau Supreme, ridden by Derek Ricketts. Beau Supreme, another horse of immense talent, cleared the big fence but Forgie did not. Next stop was Stoneleigh for the Everest Double Glazing Championships which, in those days, took place at the National Equestrian Centre.

Then the long haul down the M6 and M1 for the 1971 Horse of the Year Show. Their practices at indoor shows certainly paid off for on the Wednesday night Paddy and Pennwood Forge Mill won the Butlins Have-A-Gamble Stakes against all the experienced horses. His first win in the Wembley arena where he was to go on to delight the capacity crowds over the years. Forgie loves people and the electric atmosphere of Wembley caught his imagination.

Later that month the Pennwood contingent travelled to Leeuwarden Show in the north of Holland. Terraces with tables and chairs and colourful umbrellas lent a festive air to this well organised show but the stabling was diabolical. They were put in stalls at the local cattle market with a little rail about three foot high on which to tie them. Being cattle stalls their front feet were higher than their back on a double level, hardly suitable stabling for valuable International horses. Despite these conditions Paddy and Forgie won the Mayor's Plate, the main competition, and were placed in two other classes including the Grand Prix in which he had four faults. Sally's memory of this show is not happy for she had two lots of money stolen from her trunk. Weather conditions were appalling but Chef d'Equipe Robin Leyland coped admirably.

Geneva Show in November was next on the agenda. Travelling in Lionel Dunning's horse box they encountered troubles along the way when the lorry got very hot. Lionel opened the water tank, waiting for the burst of hot air which didn't come. So he bent forward only to be met by a jet of boiling water containing anti-freeze. It scalded poor Lionel's face and his wife Pam had to drive the rest of the way. They were due to check in at a border post in the Swiss Alps at eight o'clock in the evening but arrived five minutes late with the guards refusing to open up. So there they were in mid-winter in icy conditions with the horses having been on the lorry for two days. There was nothing for it but to leave the horses on the lorry and for humans and horses to try to get some sleep. When they awoke the next morning they were frozen, full of cramp and were horrified to discover they had gone to the wrong border post. To make matters worse the correct border post had stayed open all night waiting for them! They eventually reached Geneva at 12 noon with Forge Mill having to turn out to jump for Britain in his first class at two o'clock. After four days travelling he jumped a clear round, finishing tenth.

The fences at Geneva were vast and to make matters worse jumping conditions were very poor with a newly laid surface which was too shallow for the horses to get a secure footing. We must also remember that Forge Mill was still pretty inexperienced, only in his first International season. The courses included jumping over a bank and a table, rather like the permanent obstacles to be found at Hickstead. Forgie went well throughout the show without actually winning and put up a brilliant performance in the Nations Cup when we again had to be content with second place behind the Germans. He jumped two clear rounds but incurred just a quarter of a time fault in the second round. The only other combinations to achieve double clears were Olympic Gold Medallist Hans Winkler of Germany on Torphy, Fritz Ligges, also of Germany, and Switzerland's Monica Bachmann, though she too had time faults. This was after the course had been modified as so many Chef d'Equipes had complained it was too big.

Hans Winkler has won no less than five Olympic gold medals, four team and one individual, and is a former World and European show jumping champion. He has been one of Forge Mill's greatest admirers over the years and would often stand watching the horse. Indeed he tried to buy him in Rotterdam, having a sponsor all lined up, but Fred Hartill did not want the horse to compete against Great Britain in the Olympics, so did not accept the offer. When we met at Olympia last year Hans Winkler told me that he had always greatly admired Forge Mill and considered him to be one of the most genuine jumpers we have ever seen. Our other team members in Geneva were Harvey Smith, David Broome, Peter Robeson, Anneli Drummond-Hay and Alison Dawes, with Lionel Dunning riding as an individual. On the final day of the show winter weather came with a vengeance, bringing heavy snow.

Lionel Dunning had intended travelling on to Austria but as his horses weren't going too well decided instead to go home. So the Germans kindly offered to take Forgie on to the next port of call, Vienna. Sally, the horse and their luggage were duly despatched with the German team while Paddy and Fred Hartill flew to Austria.

The Germans travel their horses three across and Sally wasn't too happy about this as Forge Mill is a big horse and she didn't consider there was enough room for him in such a confined space for the long journey which in fact, with hold-ups, took 40½ hours. Forgie had jumped in the Grand Prix on the last day at Geneva which had finished at 12.30 a.m. The following morning they were up at 4.30 a.m., setting off at 6 a.m. That night was spent in the horse box and they continued the journey the next morning reaching the border at Salzburg at 12 noon. Here they experienced a four-and-a-half hour delay, not reaching Vienna until 10.30 p.m. Fortunately, Gerd Wiltfang's groom had sportingly put one of his horses on to another lorry so that Forgie could have two compartments and travel in comfort.

This typifies the wonderful sense of comradeship which prevails between nations in all spheres of equestrian sport, not only with the riders but behind the scenes. They are always ready to help each other out in times of trouble and Sally was very grateful to the Germans for being so kind and helpful. Once on the road the Germans kept going, very different from the English who would stop, get the horses out of the box to stretch their legs and have a bite of grass, before continuing on their way. The attitude of the foreign grooms towards their charges is in fact completely different. They probably think the English grooms are silly to lavish so much love on their charges, whilst the English consider them perhaps a little hard-hearted and uncaring, treating them more like machines. Nowadays, more and more English grooms are being lured to the Continent by the high wages offered there.

There was a happy and relaxed atmosphere in Vienna and acting Chef d'Equipe was Sally's father, Major Bob Warren, the popular Show Director at Hickstead from 1967 to 1974. Forge Mill jumped one of sixteen clear rounds in the opening competition to finish seventh and continued to go really well all week. In the Grand Prix he jumped two good clears to make it through to the final jump-off against five rivals. Drawn to go first he set a good time and was faultless. Lutz Merkel on Sir and the evergreen Bellevue ridden by Raimondo d'Inzeo of Italy both had four faults before another Italian, Graziano Mancinelli, sped round five seconds faster on Water Surfer. He in turn was beaten by the merest whisker by the last to go, Gerd Wiltfang on Dorian Grey, so Forgie finished third as he did in the Puissance.

The British riders for the unofficial team competition were Paddy on Pennwood Forge Mill, Mallowry Spens with Heart O'Corn and Ted Edgar with Everest Snaffles. At the end of the first round Britain was equal first with Italy, both on four faults, closely followed by Germany on seven. By the time it came to Forge Mill's second round it was all up to him, he had to go clear for us to win. Paddy and Forgie completed another brilliant clear round in their cool, calm manner to clinch the team victory. Although only a fairly small show all the top riders were there as Vienna is a very popular event. One drawback, however, is that there is nowhere to exercise the horses so the grooms used to get up at about 4.30 a.m. and ride them around the streets. Rather like riding around London early in the morning before the hub and din of the traffic gets underway. Stabling here was bad and Paddy and Fred Hartill had to set to work building a makeshift stable with planks of thin wood.

By now Pennwood Forge Mill and Paddy McMahon were regular members of British teams travelling abroad and were highly thought of. At the beginning of October 1971 the British Show Jumping Association announced the short list of riders and horses for the 1972 Olympic Games in Munich in August. As expected the ten named included Paddy and Pennwood Forge Mill, the others being: — Alison Dawes (The Maverick), Anneli Drummond-Hay (Sporting Ford), Graham Fletcher (Buttevant Boy), Ann Moore (April Love), Peter Robeson (Grebe), Mike Saywell (Hideaway), David Broome (Manhattan and Sportsman), Harvey Smith (Archie and Johnny Walker), and Alan Oliver (Sweep III).

Forge Mill would be only eight by the time of the Olympics. Had he enough experience to cope with the problems he would encounter over Mickey Brinckmann's big courses?

6

OLYMPIC YEAR—WOULD FORGE MILL BE CHOSEN?

One of the stipulations made when Pennwood Forge Mill was named as an Olympic possible was that his trade prefix of Pennwood should be removed, so on 8th March 1972 his name was officially changed on B.S.J.A. records to Forge Mill. Colonel (now Sir Harry) Llewellyn, chairman of our show jumping selectors, outlined the course of campaign to potential owners and riders at the beginning of March. It had been decided to cut down on the travel abroad during the first half of the season and just send a team to Aachen, where Herr Brinckmann was building the courses. Full Olympic practices for the selected horses and riders were to be held at the Bath and West Show and The Royal Highland.

Forge Mill enjoyed a nice long rest before being brought back into work in March. Soon afterwards, on the 12th, fire swept through the hayricks and buildings at Mount Farm causing £8,000 worth of damage. Forge Mill and other horses had to be led to safety and so one of the world's most valuable jumpers narrowly escaped death. Only a few months earlier Fred Hartill had been offered £50,000 for the horse from a foreign buyer but he was not interested in selling him to compete against us in Munich. It had long been Paddy's dream to ride for his country in the Olympics and he carefully prepared a schedule of shows for early 1972, it was necessary to plan way ahead.

Somewhat to the surprise of his connections Forgie was selected to travel to Rome in May with the British team. His travelling companions were Marion Mould (née Coakes) with Bandolera and Bells of Galway; Anneli Wucherpfennig (née Drummond-Hay) with Sceptre and speed merchant, Xanthos; Alan Oliver riding Sweep III and Bay Rum; Peter Robeson with Grebe and Quail and Mike Saywell riding Ten to Twelve and Able Monarch. Not really thinking that they would be chosen Forge Mill was far from fit and still carrying a lot of weight, something he is prone to at the best of times. They had a terrific job getting him fit in time and made him a special plastic sweat rug in the Pennwood workshop, to try to get his weight down. Sally spent hours each day giving Forgie his sauna bath, washing him down afterwards and drying him off thoroughly to prevent him catching cold.

He went, still in rather a podgy condition, to Rome where the courses were, as expected, rather big but he was placed in a number of classes, including fourth in the Supreme Championship. Held in the idyllic setting of the Piazza di Siena the show had attracted seven teams plus individuals from Eire, Venezuela and the Argentine. The Nations Cup was virtually a contest between ourselves and Italy, with the home side fielding their Olympic quartet of Graziano Mancinelli with Ambassador, Vittorio Orlandi on Valetta, Raimondo d'Inzeo with Fiorello and his brother Piero with Red Fox.

The course of medium severity was designed to make riders think every inch of the way. At the halfway stage Italy led Britain by one fence, with Germany third and the rest 'also rans'. But in the second round things did not go so well for our team of Anneli with Sceptre, Alan riding Sweep III,

Peter on Grebe and Paddy with Forge Mill. This was despite the fact that some members of the team had thrown coins into the reputedly lucky Trevi fountain. Forge Mill had four faults in both rounds and we finished second to the Italians.

Alan Oliver enjoyed a good show with Sweep, winning the leading foreign rider award and the Premio Campello, plus several placings. For Anneli it was a sad final appearance for Britain before settling in South Africa with her husband of a few months. She had been a great ambassador for the sport and was always particularly popular in Rome. The homeward journey took them along the attractive coastal route through Menton and Monte Carlo before stabling the horses overnight at Cagnes Racecourse. The following night was spent at Fontainebleau, the big French Equitation School, regularly used as a stopping-off post for British teams travelling through France.

The 1972 home season got off to a good start with Forge Mill winning yet another Area International Trial, this time at Aldershot where he had the only clear in the jump-off. He was also placed in A.I.T.s at Leicester and the Three Counties, winning the Gentlemen's Championship at the latter.

So to the Bath and West Show, held on their permanent showground at Shepton Mallet at the beginning of June. Forge Mill coped magnificently with a testing course which included a big treble and he proved to the selectors that he undoubtedly had scope. Paddy was well pleased with his performance for he finished second to Alan Oliver riding Mr. and Mrs. Cawthraw's Sweep III, with Graham Fletcher and Talk of the North in third place.

Paddy and Forge Mill did not take part in the Royal Highland trial where Harvey Smith's Summertime put up a good performance to win and was added to the short list. Malcolm Pyrah finished second with the former champion hack, Lucky Strike, and Graham Fletcher again third, this time with the inexperienced Brawith Park. Due to an outbreak of horse sickness it was decided not to send a team to Aachen after all and so two additional Olympic Trials were scheduled for the Great Yorkshire Show and Hickstead.

Forge Mill is always highly popular with the crowds who flock to the Royal Show at Stoneleigh and at the beginning of July he delighted them by winning the Texaco Championship. Then up to Yorkshire for the third Olympic trial. Major Reg Whitehead's course was more exacting than the previous two and the only clear came from Mike Saywell with Hideaway, who had knocked five fences down at the Royal Highland. It was at Harrogate that Forge Mill, who must have been high on the selectors' list after the Bath and West, fell from favour. Combinations have always been Forge Mill's weakness and here disaster struck for he had a refusal in the middle and then made a complete mess of it next time through. Paddy, perhaps riding over-anxiously in view of what was at stake, had asked the horse to stand back too far and it was impossible for him to make the last part. Many people felt that Paddy was riding too desperately, so keen was he to make the Olympics which is every rider's dream. When he came out of the ring Fred Hartill told him that the Olympics weren't that important. It was only Forge Mill's second season in International jumping and he was comparatively inexperienced for an Olympic horse, where knowledge counts for a lot.

So to the final trial at Hickstead, where it was obligatory for the Olympic possibles to compete. The course was considered by many experts to be of no real value in selecting the right team for Munich. Although the fences were big there is room in the Hickstead arena for so much space between them, thus making the course easier. In the Olympic stadium there would not be so much space between fences, therefore presenting far greater problems. However, the spread out of the treble was a real test of scope as was the double over the twin water ditches and the water itself at 16 ft. 4 in. wide.

Peter Robeson and Grebe charted the course and had

four fences down for 16 faults. Forge Mill had two fences on the ground for eight faults, as did The Maverick. Lucky Strike was retired, Sweep (who had by now lost his good form of earlier in the season) had 12 faults and Summertime four. The three who managed to get round unscathed were Mike Saywell with Hideaway, David Broome with Manhattan and Ann Moore with Psalm (who was now considered a better Olympic ride for her than April Love). First to go in the barrage was Manhattan, who took third place with three fences down when Hideaway and Psalm both had eight faults. Their owners did not want them to jump-off against the clock, feeling they had done enough, but the judges were adamant. Hideaway incurred eight faults in 65·3 seconds before the Warwickshire girl and Psalm also had two down but were 6·1 seconds faster to make sure of their ticket to Munich.

The selectors were Harry Llewellyn (Chairman), Pat Koechlin-Smythe, Wilf White, Gerald Barnes, George Hobbs and Ronnie Masserella (Team Manager). After a lengthy suspense, the four they selected to travel to Germany were Ann Moore (Psalm), Mike Saywell (Hideaway), Alison Dawes (The Maverick) and David Broome (Manhattan). The latter was not to my mind ideal Olympic material, for he could be very erratic, but David had no other horse to take and he was very experienced. Hideaway was undoubtedly a horse with the scope to tackle an Olympic course, he was not brilliant but he was very reliable. Much to the surprise of many people Harvey Smith was not amongst those named.

Maybe they had not forgotten Forge Mill's lapse at the Great Yorkshire, when he was in trouble at the combination, and probably considered him too inexperienced. Paddy was naturally very disappointed at not being chosen. Forge Mill was still only eight and when you look at the age of most of the show jumpers who go to the Olympics you will find that many are nearly as old or older than Forge Mill is today. For instance, Summertime was 12 in Munich,

Stroller 16 when he won his Silver Medal in Mexico in 1968, Mister Softee 14 in Mexico, Hideaway 14 at the time of the Montreal Olympics and Jacopo 11 when he took part in the Tokyo Olympics of 1964. Many of the foreign horses such as Bellevue were even older when they competed.

Fred Hartill and other owners of potential Olympic horses had been called to a meeting of the selection committee during 1972 and asked if they would be willing to lend their horses to a pool for the selected riders. First in was Fred Hartill and his answer was "No, either the horse goes to Munich with Paddy McMahon or not at all". He felt his young rider had immense talent and should be given his chance along with the horse. Besides, as we saw in Montreal in 1976, you cannot put a rider, however gifted and experienced, on a strange horse, however brilliant, a month before the Olympics and expect to win medals. We must plan ahead far more if we are to hold our own in the Moscow Olympics of 1980.

By way of consolation Paddy and Forge Mill were named for the British team at the Royal International and included in our Nations Cup team which won the Prince of Wales Cup with four faults to Italy's 28. Sharing in this fine victory were Alan Oliver with Sweep III, Harvey Smith with Mattie Brown and David Broome with Sportsman. As usual, Forgie adapted well to the confined space, so well that he and Paddy won the Saddle of Honour for the horse gaining the most number of points throughout the show. Although they didn't actually win a class, they were consistently well placed. They got under way with a fourth place in the opening night's Horse and Hound Cup, were equal second in the Puissance, fifth in the Grand Prix and third in both the King George V Gold Cup and the Daily Mail Cup, the show's Victor Ludorum. Paddy and Forge Mill had really hit the big time and could do little wrong. It was as if they were saying to the selectors, "I'll prove you wrong".

In July Alison Dawes asked the selectors to drop The Maverick from the Olympic team due to injury which had kept him short of work, and the combination of Harvey Smith and Summertime was substituted. In the Munich Individual Show Jumping it was Ann Moore and Psalm who kept the flag flying for Britain by reaching the jump-off with eight faults over the two rounds. She was certain of a medal for only two other riders had got round with so few faults — Graziano Mancinelli of Italy with his Irish-bred grey, Ambassador, and Neil Shapiro of America riding Sloopy. In the jump-off the American horse had eight faults before the Italian jumped a lovely clear on Ambassador. Ann was determined to have a go and came round the corner into the upright white rails a bit sharp with the result that Psalm stopped, but they were otherwise faultless for just three faults and the silver medal. David on Manhattan finished 14th and Mike riding Hideaway 15th.

In the team contest we were standing equal third at halfway on 23 faults, preceded by West Germany on 16 and the United States with 16·25 and were therefore still in the hunt for a medal. Summertime jumped a very good round for four faults at the second fence and Hideaway jumped another consistent round for eight faults. Psalm had lost some of his form by now and was in trouble in the combination and knocked up a cricket score. Nevertheless, our last horse, Manhattan, could afford to have three fences down and we would still win the bronze medal. But as I've said, Manhattan can be rather erratic and, losing his concentration, he had the first two and last two fences down and the bronze slipped from our grasp. Our horses and riders finished with the following scores: —

> Harvey Smith (Summertime) 16 and 4
> Mike Saywell (Hideaway) 8 and 8
> Ann Moore (Psalm) 11 and 21
> David Broome (Manhattan) 4 and 16

Meanwhile back at home Forge Mill and Paddy McMahon were enjoying a terrific run of success. He won both the Olympic Trial and the Championship at British Timken. Often the Pennwood box would be driving along and when stopped at traffic lights or in a jam complete strangers, seeing the Pennwood sign, would lean out of their car windows and say, "You should be in Munich". There was a lot of public feeling about it for he was already a firm favourite with television viewers.

The number of miles travelled each season by the show jumpers is vast. For instance, during the 1972 season Paddy and Forge Mill won the big class at Anglesey Show in Wales. Leaving the showground at 5 p.m. they reached Wolverhampton around midnight, changed the box and some of the horses and set off for Hickstead in Sussex, arriving at 10.30 a.m. the following morning. Despite having so little rest, Forge Mill won the Castella Stakes on the opening day. However, on the Friday he was off his food, as he was on Saturday, possibly because of the long journey, so Paddy decided not to jump him.

Each year at the Hickstead August meeting the British Jumping Derby is staged, with the 10 ft. 6 in. bank in action for the only time. The course is normally of some 16 fences and requires stamina, with few clear rounds having been jumped over the years. Derby morning dawned on the Sunday and Forgie had eaten some breakfast so Paddy decided to ride him round the showground to see how he felt and then make a decision as to whether to jump him. He felt in good spirits so Paddy decided to take him in the Derby. He went brilliantly, just having four faults at the first part of the Devil's Dyke. He had not jumped this before as he had been unable to compete in the Derby Trial. The gigantic bank looks formidable but over the years has caused very little trouble and horses do not, with a few exceptions, object to coming down it. I asked Sally for her feelings when her beloved Forge Mill was about to descend it and she told me, "Heart failure, I kept thinking what if he falls and gets hurt". But all was well and he didn't hesitate before tackling the big drop.

Before going to Hickstead Paddy thought they'd better give Forgie some practice over banks. So they took him on to

Penn Common, where he would have nothing to do with a deep gully, and Paddy had visions of himself being stuck on top of the Derby bank with Forgie refusing to move in either direction! They then decided to take him to Sedgley over the sheer drops of the Beacon Slopes and here he performed well up and down the steep terrain.

Forgie's performance of just four faults over the marathon Derby course was not bettered all afternoon but it was equalled by Derek Ricketts on Tyrolean Holiday and Hendrick Snoek of Germany riding Shirokko to force a jump-off. The German, going first, was clear, whilst Forgie was in the water and, going too steadily, also incurred three-quarters of a time fault to take the runners-up award when Derek's mount had two fences down.

The pre-Wembley indoor shows such as the Everest Double Glazing Championships perform a useful purpose in getting horses going well over big courses before reaching Wembley. As usual, Forge Mill competed at Stoneleigh before travelling to London, finishing second in both the Everest Double Glazing Championship and the Himalayan Championship.

It was at the 1972 Horse of the Year Show that Paddy and Forge Mill undoubtedly achieved their greatest triumph, the Ronson Trophy on the final night. Their classic round in 28·3 seconds in this Victor Ludorum had the crowd standing as Paddy set Forge Mill alight as they went through the start. Twisting like a stag, he had done the impossible and beaten Paul Schockemohle's seemingly unbeatable time by one-tenth of a second. The crowd went wild and there was hardly a dry eye in the place. The crowd's darling Pennwood Forge Mill and his handsome and talented rider Paddy McMahon had beaten the Germans.

Pennwood Forge Mill was a really great horse, he could meet a fence at speed from any angle and jump it well, turning in the air, ready for the next fence. What the crowds in the packed Empire Pool did not know was that a few minutes earlier Forge Mill had slipped at the practice fence in the outside collecting ring and fallen in the wet conditions. With the strict timetable at Wembley there was no time to wash his mouth out properly so he had to jump his winning round with black cinders in his mouth.

Everybody rushed off to the reception given after this class and it was one of Forge Mill's greatest fans, Peter Robeson, who came to help Sally take his bandages off. He's always had a soft spot for the horse.

There had been a lot of talk in the Press at this time that Fred Hartill was thinking of selling Pennwood Forge Mill and Fred admits that the money was tempting and he did consider it. As the jubilant owner ran down the steps to the collecting ring after his Ronson Trophy win a little old lady rushed up to him and said, with tears streaming down her face, "Please don't sell him, Mr. Hartill". The following day Fred Hartill was offered a lot of money for Forgie, both from foreign buyers and the home market. It was a temptation but everybody threatened to leave him if he sold Forge Mill so he decided against it!

To crown a memorable week at Wembley he was also second in the Sunday Times Cup and the Norwich Union Stakes, the Puissance event. He had, in fact, a very good record in test competitions, always finishing in the top few. His highest jump was 7 ft. 3 in. which he cleared in Vienna in 1975. He also went to Vienna in 1972 when we again won the unofficial team competition. Forgie was also equal first in the Puissance and second in the opening competition.

Paddy and Forge Mill had not reached their goal of the Olympic Games but things had gone very well at home. Had the Olympics been a year later Forge Mill would undoubtedly have made the team for he was improving all the time. Youth was not on his side on this occasion. When the B.S.J.A. published their list of Top Twenty Horses at the end of the 1972 season, both the National and International tables were headed by Pennwood Forge Mill, his combined total being over £1,300 higher than his nearest rival. He and Paddy had reached the top.

7

THE HISTORY OF PENNWOOD

We pause now from the story of Pennwood Forge Mill's ups and downs and take a look at the origin of Pennwood and the history of the Hartill family, which is steeped in horses and show jumping.

Fred Hartill's grandfather owned a string of colleries in Sedgley which worked 110 pit ponies, some of which Fred rode as a child. His father's main occupation was a string of butcher's shops but his hobby was breaking and dealing in horses. Fred himself went into the butchers' trade and his brother Bill still runs the shops in Sedgley.

When I asked Fred how long he'd been with horses, he replied, "I was with horses before I was born because my father went to sell a horse to my grandfather and met my mother!". His grandfather and father both shared a passion for Stepping Cobs, the old type of Welsh Cob which stepped rather like a hackney pony and had hair in his heel, and showed them at agricultural shows. One day his father bought the Champion Tradesman's Turnout at a show for £35, a lot of money in those days. It was a Palomino Welsh Cob standing 14.3 h.h. and was docked and hogged. Fred was warned not to tell his mother how much it had cost but she eventually found out and told him he must be mad!

Just before the outbreak of the war in 1937 Fred and his father went off to the New Forest on a buying spree. They came back with two truck loads of two-year-olds (to make 14.2 h.h. ponies) costing the princely sum of 27s. 6d. each. The same day they also bought a load of weaned foals at ten shillings each which seems difficult to believe in these days of inflated prices.

At the age of seven Fred had what he describes as a minor serious accident, riding not a pony but a sheep! His father was a regular worshipper at Sedgley Church where he sung in the choir and the vicar asked him if he would put some sheep into the more or less disused cemetery to eat the grass down. As they were putting them in young Fred decided to catch one to ride. The sheep bolted with the result that both sheep and Fred disappeared down an open vault, fortunately without injury to either!

From his early days of riding pit ponies Fred progressed on to some of the driving cobs being schooled by his father and taught them to jump. They then took the more promising ones to shows which were very primitive compared with today's standards. You didn't have to wear hard hats and it was in fact just after the war that the B.S.J.A. brought in the rule making the wearing of hats compulsory. The good horses of those days might not have been able to cope with the courses encountered today. They were brilliant at jumping straight up and down but may not have been able to adapt to jumping big spreads. When the clock was introduced in the '50s many of the old show jumpers were against it, they preferred the method of reaching a decision by slats on the top of fences without rushing against time.

Fred caught the dealing bug at the very early age of 11. He saw a pony advertised for sale in the local paper, together with a flat (a single-axle two-wheeled cart) and set of harness. So he set off on his bike to see the turnout, discovering that the vendor wanted £15 for it. This was beyond his means so, being a shrewd businessman even in those early days, offered £11 which was accepted. He brought the pony home, schooled it to jump and took it to Bromsgrove Fair where he made £13 10s. of it, £7 for the newly painted flat and £1 for the set of harness — not a bad start for one so young, a profit of £10.

His brother then decided to go into partnership with him and the pair bought a 11.2 h.h. pony, a 13.2 h.h. pony and a 14.2 h.h. pony for £12 10s. the three. All were somewhat dodgy characters for they had been broken too quickly. They set to work improving the trio, with the black 14.2 h.h. developing into a nice pony which sold for £15, receiving an old cob in part exchange which they allowed £3 on. This was later sold on to some gypsies for £7. They sold the small pony for £7 10s. and the 13.2 h.h. made £11. So they had a good deal for starters and went on dealing quietly as a sideline. Mind you, even before the pony-dealing days the boys had dealt in rabbits and guinea pigs at school, often on hire purchase!

On leaving school Fred went into the butchering trade but it was natural with his flair for dealing that he should also follow in his father's footsteps, breaking, schooling and selling horses and ponies from the stables at Sedgley Bullring. During the war he served in Burma and India for five-and-a-half years and on being demobbed came back into horses, although still continuing his work in the butcher's shop. His first purchase after the war cost £27 and was a seven-year-old standing 16.3 h.h. This he schooled and sold on for a profit, going to an auction with the proceeds and buying three more so he was soon back in business. Realising that more people were going into show jumping he decided to concentrate more on these rather than hunters as in the past.

Driving back from Cambridge Horse Sales one day he heard that Jack Skidmore and Curly Beard had a mare for sale which they were finding difficult to ride. So he called in and gave them £50 for the previously mentioned Bay Bibi, who as we know turned out to be such a find for Fred.

In those days people thought nothing of riding 30 miles to shows but gradually mechanisation began to creep in. In the middle '50s he jumped Bay Bibi at her first B.S.J.A. affiliated show, at Wombourne, where she won the open jumping. The new rule making the wearing of hats compulsory had just been brought in so Fred had to hunt round the show but all he could borrow was a pork pie hat. A spectator arriving late at the show asked a friend who had won the class, the reply being "Some foreign looking man in a funny hat!" It was around this time that the B.S.J.A. banned rapping and got much stricter with various rules which Fred considers was all for the good of the sport.

Although horses were a hobby, Fred and his brother put an enormous amount of hard work into them. One night they were attending a church social at Sedgley when some local girls suggested they start a riding school as they were having to travel some distance to the nearest one. After due consideration they thought this a sound idea and started off modestly with four cobs. This soon snowballed and within weeks they were getting dozens of riders. By the time they moved to Mount Farm, Penn, they had 47 horses operating from the stables behind the shops in Sedgley, now a bustling town centre.

During the course of escorting rides Fred Hartill and his wife Janet would often ride past Mount Farm, set high on the edge of Penn Common. The farm had been empty for some 12 months and houses built on part of the land. The firm concerned then decided to sell off the farm house, out-buildings (consisting of cow houses, four stables, a dutch type piggery for 250 and some old style piggeries), plus 42 acres, by public auction. One day as they rode past, Fred and Janet noticed that the auction was later that day. Fred remarked it would be an ideal spot for them being on the edge of Penn Common with plenty of hacking land. Mrs. Hartill agreed but pointed out it would need a lot of work on it.

50

Fred nearly forgot about the auction so busy was he in the shop but he remembered in the nick of time and he and Bill rushed to the Star and Garter Hotel in Wolverhampton, put in a bid and secured the property. When he went home and broke the news to his wife over a cup of tea it did not receive the most enthusiastic reception.

On surveying their purchase the following day they found that Mrs. Hartill was right, there was a lot of work to be done. Fortunately many of the Sedgley riders gathered up tools and paint brushes to help with the decorating and alterations and the school opened its doors on Whit-Saturday 1956 with 50 riders.

The riding school grew and grew until they had 500 riders per week. In 1971 when Pennwood Forge Mill was becoming popular it was decided to discontinue the riding school as it was not making a profit and concentrate on producing better class horses and ponies for selling. Fred enjoyed training children and watching them improve and missed that side of things. In fact, they all found it rather quiet for the first few weeks.

Never one to miss a chance, even at Sedgley they had sold riding wear to the riders for they had to buy it somewhere, why not on the premises? As the dealing side grew they were constantly being asked where they could buy saddles and bridles for the horses they'd just bought. So Fred Hartill decided to set up an establishment selling everything from a hoof pick to a horse, a whip to a stable, a tail bandage to a saddle — in fact there's little you can't buy at Pennwood. He also employs qualified saddlers to make the famous Pennwood range, such as the Pennwood Lightweight and the Colton, although much of the work still has to be contracted out. In the old days they used the hides from the butchers' shops but this has now been discontinued.

The business is now vast with 90% of the trade being export, to some 28 countries. Approximately 75 horses are normally for sale at any one time. From these are selected the ones most likely to make show jumpers and these are then transferred to Valerie Hartill's yard of ten boxes. Here they are schooled thoroughly before being taken to shows, either by Valerie or Geoff Glazzard, provided they can use themselves over a course of fences. There are plenty of horses which can jump one fence well but it's often a different matter to find one with the ability to jump a course.

But for all the stars there are many more who don't make the grade. As Fred Hartill rightly says, "You go prospecting to find the diamond and he is the one who's got to pay for the others you've handled who didn't make it". The ones not so likely to make show jumpers are schooled and sold on as hacks or hunters.

"A good show jumper today is an unusual combination because he's got to have the ability to fire himself over five-foot parallels and the temperament to stay in your hand and wait for the signal to go. Besides ability he must have an international brain to really make the grade." This is Fred Hartill's theory on a top class show jumper.

Valerie Hartill produces many young show jumpers from the Pennwood yard. She finds a horse she likes only to have it sold on, very often abroad. Out of the 21 horses she jumped last season 20 went overseas, for it is the foreign buyers who can afford the big money. But Valerie accepts it all philosophically with a smile, for dealing has always been part of the Hartill life. She started riding at the age of three, one of her first mounts being Forge Mill's devoted companion, Magpie.

There is great hustle and bustle in the yard at Pennwood, the shop is always full and on one of my many visits eight horses were sold during the course of the afternoon and three Masters of Hounds came seeking mounts for the coming season. The happy staff underline their loyalty to the Hartills by the fact that many stay for years. Valerie's brother Stephen Hartill manages the shop, which has a staff of six, and generally holds the fort when they are away on the show circuit. He used to ride as a child, having a natural

1. A picture of happiness as Forgie and Valerie enjoy themselves cantering up the steep slopes behind Pennwood.

2.
Arksey and
Forge Mill out
exercising with
Valerie around
the lanes of Penn
Common.

3. Mrs. Hartill gives Forgie his daily apple. He won't go past the door unless he gets his titbit and prefers 'Granny Smiths'!

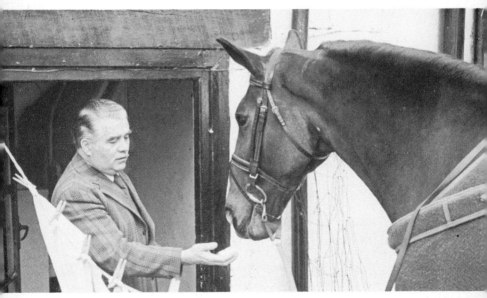

4. Not to be outdone Arksey, who joined the Pennwood string in 1978, has to have his apple from Fred Hartill.

5. Fred Hartill competed in show jumping events for many years and is seen here jumping Pennwood Gold Flake at her first show.

6. When Forge Mill first arrived at Pennwood Graham Terry would lower himself on to his back from the beams above his stall.

7. John Wrathall and Forge Mill competing in their first Area International Trial at Leicester County Show in June 1970 when they finished equal fifth. John, a Northamptonshire farmer, jumped Forge Mill for three seasons.

8.
A happy Paddy McMahon poses with his great favourite Pennwood Forge Mill.

9. Their first trip abroad and Pennwood Forge
Mill and Paddy McMahon cover themselves
in glory by winning the Ostend Grand Prix.
They were put on the short list for the
Munich Olympics soon afterwards.

10. Nations Cup line-up in Dublin 1973 when we won the Aga
Khan Trophy with a zero score.
l. to r.: Peter Robeson on Grebe; Paddy on Pennwood Forge
Mill; David Broome on Manhattan; Ann Moore on Psalm.

11. The European Crown — Paddy McMahon and Pennwood Forge Mill receive their rosette from H.R.H. Prince Philip after their great victory in the 1973 European Championships at Hickstead.

12. "Thank You For Looking After Me." Forgie shows his appreciation to Sally Warren, his groom for three years.

13. Her Majesty The Queen talking to Paddy McMahon and owner Fred Hartill after Forgie had won the 1973 King George V Gold Cup. This was a proud moment for all concerned.

14. Paddy and Pennwood Forge Mill jumping to victory in the **King George V Gold Cup** at Wembley.

15 (a, b, c).
The 10 ft. 6 in. Derby
Bank at Hickstead
presents no problem to
Paddy McMahon and
Forge Mill. They were
unlucky not to win in
1972, finishing second
to Hendrick Snoek of
Germany riding
Shirokko.

16. "Just the right size for me" — one of Mrs. Hartill's Pomeranian dogs sits in the Horse and Hound Cup won by Pennwood Forge Mill in 1973 and again in 1978.

17.
Monty, one of our best-known equestrian photographers before his retirement a few years ago, achieves one of his ambitions — to ride Forge Mill.

18. Forgie, with his rider and owner, admires the lovely Irish Horse Board Trophy he won during the 1973 season.

19. Enjoying a well-earned rest in his paddock, Forgie and his devoted companion Magpie.

20. "Who do you think will win tomorrow?" — Pennwood Forge Mill and Lavandel, ridden by Hugo Simon, seem to be discussing their chances after the second leg of the World Championships at Hickstead in 1974.

21. Pennwood Forge Mill, ridden by Paddy McMahon, puts in a perfect leap at Hickstead to demonstrate how water should be jumped.

22. Geoff Glazzard rides Forge Mill to victory in the Radio Rentals Stakes at the Bath and West Show.

23. Recently completed at Pennwood is Forgie's own special suite. It has a stable, wash box and a room showing some of his photographs and rosettes.

24. Michael Clayton, editor of 'Horse & Hound', presents the Horse and Hound Cup to Geoff Glazzard on Pennwood Forge Mill.

25. Geoff and Forge Mill en route to a win in the 1978 Horse and Hound Cup, they jumped a clear round in 33·7 seconds.

26. Outside the shop at Pennwood, Forgie with Val, Mrs. Hartill and Stephen (Mr. Hartill has gone missing!). Behind can be seen the window displaying some of his many trophies.

27. Valerie and Forgie enjoy a break at home between shows.

28. Geoff Glazzard and Forge Mill taking part in the jump-off for the Harris Carpets Stakes at Olympia in which they finished fifth.

29. Proud owner Fred Hartill stands beside Pennwood Forge Mill, ridden by his daughter Valerie, before the presentation of the President's Trophy at Olympia 1978.

30.
Watched by a packed house Forgie, ridden by Geoff Glazzard, puts in a great leap at the 1978 Olympia Christmas Show.

31. Pennwood Forge Mill and Paddy McMahon sail over one of Hickstead's water ditches to land one of their biggest wins — the 1973 European Championship.

eye, but then gave it up until, suddenly left without a stable jockey at short notice, he took over the ride on the horses. At Kenilworth Show he jumped two clear rounds on Pennwood Gold Flake and did well with the novice horses. Not having done any jumping for a number of years he's recently caught the bug again and has been taking some novices to a few shows. Mrs. Hartill is kept busy doing the entries and preparing a seemingly unending supply of delicious food for all the staff, many of whom live in.

Amongst the good horses produced from Pennwood have been Koyli, a horse which went well for Paddy McMahon before being sold to Belgium and then on to Austria; Logic, who went to Liz Clewer and was, says Fred Hartill, "One I should never have sold"; Pepperpot, on which Gill Kelly won the Individual Bronze Medal and Team Gold at the 1978 Junior European Show Jumping Championships; Kilbrin and Carnaby, to mention but a few. Also the promising Drumandora, a seven-year-old standing only 15.2 h.h. but considered by Fred to be one of the best small ones he's ever had. Ridden by Geoff Glazzard she finished second in the 1977 Foxhunter Championship at Wembley.

Fred himself, as you've discovered, is no stranger to show jumping, having competed from 1949 until he had to give up in 1965 having broken his neck on three occasions. One of his best mounts was Pennwood Gold Flake, taken over by Paddy McMahon as a Grade 'A' when he rejoined Pennwood from Trevor Banks.

Visitors to Pennwood Saddlery also hope, of course, for a glimpse of the famous Pennwood Forge Mill. Another attraction is the aviary housing some 300 birds and the pet fox called Vicki. There are always plenty of dogs around the place for Mrs. Hartill breeds Pomeranians and there is dear old Henry, the 14-year-old brown and white border collie, who, although now pensioned off, still likes to help load a pony, and his half brother Jason. There are also some 300 pigeons, including the Medina variety, around the yard which makes the horses used to sudden movements and flapping. Being forever commercially minded even these are for sale to pay their way!

Fred's father instilled into his sons the following theory — everything you've got is for improving and taking profit. So if anybody offers you profit you should ask yourself if you would give that much for it. If the answer is no then you should sell it. Fred Hartill has heeded this advice and the only things he won't sell are Pennwood Forge Mill and his wife!

8

THE EUROPEAN CROWN

1973 was to prove a marvellous year for the partnership of
Pennwood Forge Mill and Paddy McMahon, little could go
wrong for them. On 9th February 1973 Paddy was one of
our first riders to turn professional, therefore debarring him
from the Olympics. They spent much of the year travelling
abroad representing Great Britain at various international
shows. After a visit to the Easter Hickstead meeting, they
kicked off as they were to go on with a win in the Area
International Trial at Newark and Notts Show in May, the
horses being stabled with Belvoir Hunt secretary and well-
known commentator Tom Hudson. This was followed by
Royal Windsor where they took second place in the A.I.T.
and two other events. In fact, at this time it was history when
the pair had a fence down, so consistent were they. Again,
with the European Championships in sight, a special
campaign had to be thought out and if the going was too
heavy Forgie was not jumped.

At the end of May they travelled to Madrid, taking the
horse-boxes to Dunkirk before boarding the train for the re-
mainder of the journey. They reached the Spanish border in

good time, travelling in fairly comfortable French-style trains. Here, though, they were switched on to cattle trucks as the French vans were too wide for the Spanish tracks. Sally was in one cattle truck with Forgie and Paddy's other mount, Pennwood Millbridge, together with supplies of food for both herself and the horses. It was very dangerous for there was no communication with the outside world, no lights, nothing. All very alarming as they were hitched on to the back of a high speed passenger train and the whip-lash effect was incredible. Fortunately, Forge Mill and Millbridge travelled well but some of the other grooms were not so lucky and had a very unpleasant time trying to give their horses tranquilising injections in pitch darkness to try to calm them as the train rocked from side to side at approximately 80 miles per hour. Paddy was also on the train and found it very difficult to get any sleep with the train rocking so.

During the journey Malcolm Pyrah's mount Trevarrion developed azoturia and Paddy was on hand to give it an injection which put it back on the road to recovery. Paddy himself caught a Spanish tummy during the journey and when the other riders arrived, one of them, George Hobbs, suggested they had a meal at a little Spanish place he knew just around the corner. The others tucked into a delicious dinner but poor Paddy couldn't eat a thing and had to keep leaving the room — much to the amusement of his team mates! But the boot was on the other foot when the following day they all went down with Spanish tummy!

The grooms and horses, plus Paddy, had arrived in Madrid in record time but feeling extremely shaken. When they saw the British Ambassador, Sir John Russell, they asked him if he could arrange for them to be put on a slower train for the homeward journey. He was very helpful and arranged that they should be hitched on to the back of a goods train. The journey to the French border took three days with the train chugging up and down Spain and taking them through the canyons of the cowboy country. They hadn't been warned that the journey would take so long and were unprepared and had only brought food and water for two days. It was a complete nightmare as it was very hot and most of the grooms developed Spanish tummy.

Eventually they reached the French border, where, to make matters worse, they were left sitting in a siding for a day and a half. But these hold-ups become second nature to the show jumping and eventing grooms for it happens so often when they are travelling abroad and somehow they always manage to cope. They were finally transferred on to a French train and transported to Paris through the main passenger station. Here, opening the doors to get some fresh air for themselves and the horses, they found the French commuters peering in at them as, looking decidedly hot and scruffy, they hungrily devoured their last tin of baked beans!

Another unpleasant incident occurred during this same trip. On reaching Dunkirk they discovered they didn't have a proper ramp to take the horses off the train, so they put the horse-boxes on a ramp and found a forklift truck with a wooden platform so that they could walk the horses from the train across the platform on to the lorry. Rather a precarious adventure not to be lightly undertaken with so much valuable horse flesh at stake. With her heart in her mouth Sally put Forgie on to the platform but he refused to come off. Although he travels well, he does tend to panic in an unusual situation such as this. The platform was about ten feet off the ground and wasn't very stable and Forgie was suspended there for a good five minutes. He kept going back with one hind leg slipping off the edge. It was very worrying for Sally and they decided to get him back on to the train, which they eventually accomplished. They then had to move the train and unload him down a very steep slope.

The other members of our team in Madrid were Malcolm Pyrah, Ann Backhouse, George Hobbs and Ray Howe. When they finally reached home soil they were greeted by George Hobbs saying, "I told you we should have flown the horses there". Anyway, despite all the problems and Spanish tummies the trip to Spain was worthwhile as Forge Mill and Paddy won three classes, including the Grand Prix, and were second in two others. We also won the Nations Cup, although the opposition was very poor. This show is held in the beautiful grounds of the Club de Campo on the outskirts of the city and took place under a scorching sun.

From the excitements of Spain they travelled straight to the South of England Show at Ardingly in Sussex, where Forgie was fifth in his class after his long and arduous journey. He performed brilliantly at the Nottinghamshire Show Jumping Spectacular at the end of June to win the John Player Grand Prix.

It was hardly surprising that, after going so well all season, Paddy and Pennwood Forge Mill should be chosen at a meeting of the selectors on 9th July to represent their country in the European Show Jumping Championships taking place at Hickstead. Paddy's second string was to be Pennwood Millbridge, formerly called Regal Kane when jumped by Sarah Roger-Smith. In my opinion he was not up to the task in hand.

There was a moment at the Royal Show at Stoneleigh at the beginning of July when it looked as though all the hard work and anticipation would come to nothing. The first two days' jumping had been dominated by Forge Mill, he won both the Texaco Trophy and the Dunhill Trophy and was given a well-earned rest on the Wednesday. In the following day's B.M.W. Championship he and Paddy reached the jump-off once more. Going well and still clear they turned sharp right-handed into a big rustic triple. Paddy can remember seeing something flapping behind the horse and the next moment they were both on the floor in a heap. When he picked himself up Paddy rushed over to the judges' box and complained, for it was a timing wire which they'd tripped over and it should not have been there. Captain Jack Webber, the popular Secretary General of B.S.J.A. for 26 years, was one of the judges and asked Paddy what he wanted to do. Paddy said he'd like to have another go and this was allowed. Paddy told me that he went twice as fast as before but half-way through his round the ringside clock stopped, so the crowd, who were all for him, did not know his time. Then came the official announcement that he had failed by just two-tenths of a second to catch Derek Ricketts and Beau Supreme — such is the courage of the horse. Sally's thoughts as she watched in horror were that the horse was injured and would be unable to take part in the European Championships after all but fortunately both he and Paddy lived to fight another day.

And so to Hickstead, scene of the 1973 European Show Jumping Championships at Dougie Bunn's permanent course in Sussex, some ten miles from Brighton. Our other representative was the in-form Harvey Smith riding Hideaway and the German-bred Salvador III, with Malcolm Pyrah as reserve rider. After the disappointment of being left out of the Munich Olympic squad the previous year, Forge Mill's connections were really looking forward to a crack at the European title. Paddy felt Forge Mill was in tip-top form, absolutely ready for these big championships.

First leg was a speed event against the clock over a long and tough course of 15 fences, including a double and treble. The favourite, Alwin Schockemöhle of West Germany, was drawn first on Weiler and was round clear in 91·6 seconds. Paddy was feeling rather despondent as he rode into the arena, second to go, he would never beat that time. But he went even better to record one of only six clear rounds in the time of 90·7 seconds. Great Britain were in the lead and none of the 29 contenders who followed could match the speed and accuracy of Forge Mill and Weiler. In third and fourth places came Vittorio Orlandi of Italy with his two horses, Fiorello and Fulmer Feather Duster. Britain's other representative, Harvey Smith, was in eighth place with Hideaway. Paddy's second mount, Pennwood Millbridge, rather out of his depth, had a run-out and six fences down.

The European Championships were run on a points basis, with one point for first, two for second, three for third, and so on. At the end of the first leg it had therefore developed into a needle match between Paddy with one point and the German ace, Alwin Schockemöhle, on two. But it doesn't pay to be complacent, for the situation can alter dramatically from day to day and hopes fade or rise as the case may be. One bad round could drop Paddy right out of contention. In the evenings Paddy wanted no part in the festivities, preferring to have a quiet meal and an early night so as to be in top form for the following day.

The course set by Pam Carruthers for the following day's Nations Cup type event over two rounds was a big one as was to be expected with the cream of Europe taking part. The treble caused a lot of grief and the fact there was only one clear round throughout underlines the severity of the course. This came, in the first round, from our own Harvey Smith on Hideaway, but his chances evaporated when they had four fences down in the second round. Forge Mill, with four faults in the first round, was lying equal second with several others and at this stage the Championships were still wide open. The atmosphere was electric as Paddy and Forge Mill came into the enormous arena just as the weather began to deteriorate. They hit the upright poles coming out of the double (fence three), were clear at the fearful treble, but had the wall down at the second last for eight faults and a grand total over the two rounds of 12. The cheerful French rider Hubert Parot and Tic had just one fence down to add to their first round score of four and thus ran out the winners of the second leg on eight faults. Disaster overtook Alwin Schockemöhle and Rex the Robber when he turned a complete somersault at the water in appalling weather conditions which put them out of the running.

Very much in the hunt as the third day dawned were Paddy McMahon and Pennwood Forge Mill, despite their 12 faults which placed them equal second in the second leg with five others. They had a two point clear lead over Vittorio Orlandi of Italy (7·5), followed by Hugo Simon of Austria (8·5), Paul Weier of Switzerland (10·5), Hubert

Parot of France (11), with Harvey Smith in sixth place on 11·5.

Saturday was rest day with the third contest over two rounds taking place on Sunday. Forge Mill jumped well in the first round over 18 fences for four faults at the double of water ditches, a fence he is not very keen on at Hickstead. At the end of the first round it was again Harvey Smith who led the field on Hideaway. However, as on Friday, they crumpled in the second round and dropped to fifth place.

The pressure increased on Paddy when Schockemöhle and Rex the Robber were fast and faultless, as was his compatriot Fritz Ligges. So tight were the marks that one mistake from Forge Mill would have pushed him right down the line.

Paddy kept his cool and, riding with great flair and confidence, sent Forge Mill round in grand style, not quite as fast as his German rival but good enough for second place in the third leg and the European title. As they approached the big combination, clear so far, Paddy can remember thinking, "All I've got to do is jump this and the final fence and we've won". This they did and Paddy threw his arms around Forgie's neck as they went through the finish, he was so thrilled.

The grand total over the three days for Pennwood Forge Mill and Paddy was 7¼ points and in second place was the popular Alwin Schockemöhle (14), with Hubert Parot of France third (15). Our other rider, Harvey Smith, finished sixth. It had been so tense from start to finish. Being in the lead from the first day increases the pressure, it is always harder to stay in front than to come from behind — you have more to lose.

So Paddy McMahon and Pennwood Forge Mill were the kings of Europe, they had been given their chance and had won the crown. H.R.H. Prince Philip, as president of the F.E.I., presented the trophy to the pair who were probably the most popular combination in British jumping at the time, so their victory could not have been more welcome.

The hero's reception they received on returning home to Wolverhampton was fantastic, they were the toast of the locality and got a bigger cheer than Wolves!

But before they returned to Pennwood there was the Royal International Horse Show at Wembley. They drove to London the following morning and, riding on the crest of a wave, Paddy and Forge Mill won the Horse and Hound Cup on the opening night of the show. Adapting quickly to the tight turns cf the restricted Empire Pool, they twisted, turned and leapt with precision to beat Ann Moore (Britain's reigning Women's European Champion) on Psalm by 1·3 seconds. The lovely gold trophy was received from Lord Mais, the Lord Mayor of London, accompanied by the paper's editor at the time Mr. Walter Case.

Tuesday was rest day before a cut at the coveted King George V Gold Cup on Wednesday evening. This is the competition all the riders are hoping to win; it may not carry the greatest prize money but it is a prestige class. Forgie and Paddy duly reached the final where he jumped another marvellous clear round to win from the only other finalist Hans Winkler with Torphy who had four faults. This was the first year that the owner of the winning horse was presented to Her Majesty The Queen in the ring, in addition to the rider. It was a very proud Fred Hartill who accompanied an equally proud Paddy McMahon to meet the Queen, a moment to be remembered. The Queen said to them, "I've watched Pennwood Forge Mill so many times and we were all hoping he'd win as he's so popular. You must be very proud of him". For Paddy, groom Sally Warren and everybody connected with the horse, this victory and his win in the Horse and Hound Cup were sweeter than his European title, as the tension was less. Paddy was the first professional to win the King George V trophy.

By now everybody knew Pennwood Forge Mill as he walked proudly into the ring, he didn't have to be an-nounced, the crowd went really wild so popular were the combination. The reception they received from the crowd was phenomenal, his record of a European Championship, Horse and Hound Cup and King George V Gold Cup in six short days would not easily be equalled let alone broken.

After Wembley they were invited to compete at Belfast Show. Fred Hartill was keen for him to go, as was Paddy, but the B.S.J.A. weren't too happy about it because of the risk and the fact he was jumping in the British team in Dublin the following week. However, they were persuaded and Forgie enjoyed a great welcome in the land from whence he had come some six years previously.

On the day Paddy and John Greenwood arrived Paddy collapsed in the hotel and couldn't stand up. Paul Darragh's father, who is a doctor, was fortunately there at the time and diagnosed nervous exhaustion, putting it down to the tension and excitement of the past few weeks. However, Paddy recovered enough to jump and enjoyed a good show, winning the Puissance and being second in the Grand Prix.

From Belfast Forgie and Millbridge travelled south to the unique Dublin Horse Show to join the rest of the British team. Here at Ballsbridge, where the cream of Ireland's horses are gathered together, Forge Mill did not go particularly well although he was placed in several classes. However, in the Aga Khan Trophy (Nations Cup) he really proved his worth by jumping two clears in the magnificent Ballsbridge arena. Ann Moore with Psalm and David Broome with Manhattan also jumped double clears and Peter Robeson and Grebe were clear first time and not required to jump a second time as the Germans could not catch us. They finished with 16¼ faults to our zero score.

Paddy won the Top Score class on his second string Pennwood Millbridge and to round off a good week for the British team Graham Fletcher and Tauna Dora won the Six Bars competition. A nice touch here was that the Irish Army grooms had prepared a special shavings box for Forgie after Sally had mentioned at Hickstead that he had to be bedded on them as he ate his straw.

Back to Hickstead for the British Derby Meeting, Forge Mill finished equal second with Paul Schockemöhle (Alwin's brother) on Abadir, Malcolm Pyrah with Trevarrion and Eddie Macken and Oatfield Hills, just tipping the second fence (white parallels) on the marathon course. The winner was Alison Dawes riding Mr. Banbury (better known as The Maverick) who recorded the only clear of the day.

Forgie by this time was, of course, also well known abroad and accepted as one, if not *the*, leading horse in the world. Off on his travels again, this time in David Broome's box, the next stop was Rotterdam.

Again he performed well, having four faults and eight in the Nations Cup for which nine teams competed; once more we finished second to Germany. It was at Rotterdam that the girl chauffeurs who ferried the foreign teams around kept asking Fred Hartill and Paddy if they would teach them to ride. Fred and Paddy said they would teach them if they came to England. This went on throughout the show. Then, on the last day there was a special demonstration by two girls doing trick riding. Guess who they were? The two chauffeurs who had been asking them to teach them to ride — somebody else had been taken for a ride!

Next port of call was St. Gallen in Switzerland, travelling on in David Broome's lorry. This show was designed for champions and Forgie and Paddy won the Champion of Champions award and another class. Debbie Johnsey, who went on to be fourth in the Individual Show Jumping at the Montreal Olympics, was the leading lady rider and received as her prize a huge box of beautiful St. Gallen lace. This is a lovely show, timed to coincide with the annual town festival. The streets look very colourful decorated with flowers and there is music and dancing in the streets. Each one is named after a country such as England, Germany, etc., and served food and drink appropriate to their particular country at the little street restaurants which abounded. As the bands went on all night there was little chance for sleep even if you did want it!

Lister Welch's show staged on the Great Yorkshire Showground at Harrogate took place on 15th September and following a week's rest Forge Mill was feeling very fit. He twisted and turned easily over Reg Whitehead's course to win the main event.

By the Horse of the Year Show at the beginning of October Forgie had been through a long season and a little of the sparkle had gone. It wasn't one of his better shows but even so he wound up fourth in the Sunday Times Cup on the Friday evening.

After nearly a month's rest the pair travelled to Amsterdam, where they won a class. Sally and Forgie, together with Paddy's second string, Millbridge, travelled out in the Johnsey's new box. Sally was thankful for all the facilities in it for Amsterdam is renowned for being bad, with no hot water or showers and nowhere for the grooms to sleep. Liz Edgar and Everest Boomerang were our only winners here, although Paddy and Forge Mill finished third in a hard fought Grand Prix.

From Amsterdam they were to travel on to Geneva and it had been arranged that Caroline Bradley's box should pick them up for the journey to Switzerland. What they hadn't realised was that, as at most big shows, as soon as the show finished the temporary stabling would be removed. So there were Forge Mill and Millbridge stuck in the middle of this big hall with their pallet stables round them while the rest were demolished with big tractors and JCB's.

Sally waited and waited and still nobody came, for the box had been held up by high seas. Eventually Sally and the horses were taken to the Heineken Brewery Stables. She was very worried for nobody spoke a word of English and she thought that Caroline's grooms would be unable to find her. She didn't dare leave the stables although she was starving and all there was in evidence was a fridge piled high with Heineken beer!

All was well for Caroline's box finally arrived and they all met up to continue the journey to Geneva. It was cold but

Sally kept reassuring the other grooms they'd be nice and warm and stationed in a hotel in Gevena as she had been last time. But alas, on arrival they found they had been put in dormitory accommodation which, although warm, did not have any hot water. Very often at foreign shows there is nowhere to take the horses for a bite of grass but at Geneva there is a park conveniently situated opposite the stables, which are underground rows of stalls. There is a very limited practice area. In Geneva hospitality abounds and there is always a busy social life with receptions each night. The jumping goes on very late until 1 or 2 a.m. in the morning and Geneva has a reputation for formidable and original courses. Our other team members were Liz and Ted Edgar, John Greenwood, Ray Howe and Malcolm Pyrah, and although we managed a couple of seconds we did not have a win. Liz Edgar was, however, Leading Lady Rider and we finished third in the Nations Cup, with Forge Mill jumping a double clear. The only other horse to do this being the late Hartwig Steenken's Simona (Forgie's girl-friend).

One problem they have with Forgie is that he loves to eat his bed. In fact, he used to prefer straw to his feed. So they have to bag shavings from Pennwood and take them with them to shows, even when travelling abroad. This can prove very trying, especially when reaching a show late at night. They then have to take up the straw, unbag the shavings and put them down before Forgie can be installed. Then if they are travelling on the next morning they have to be up an hour earlier than everybody else in order to bag up all the shavings again. Forgie will sulk for hours if tied up so he can't eat his straw, so it is worth taking shavings despite all the extra work involved.

Forgie's final show at the end of such a memorable and successful year was the Dunhill Olympia where, to crown a fantastic season, he was second in the Turkey Stakes to David Broome and Sportsman and also in the £4,000 Victor Ludorum in which he reached the jump-off before conceding victory to Graham Fletcher and Buttevant Boy.

In 1972 the Irish Horse Board presented a lovely trophy to the Irish-bred horse winning the most number of points in International competitions during the year. The winner in the inaugural year was Graziano Mancinelli's Ambassador. Not surprisingly the 1973 award went to Pennwood Forge Mill, the Irish horse of unknown origin who had come from nowhere to triumph over his more aristocratic relations.

9

SO TO THE WORLD CHAMPIONSHIPS

1973 had been such a fantastic year, a fairy tale come true. The horse that cost a mere £130 had landed the European crown and the much-sought-after King George V Gold Cup during a season when he had captured so many awards and could do little wrong.

Could the success story continue in 1974, the year of the important World Show Jumping Championships? Last season would be very hard to follow. The Championships were due to take place at Hickstead in July by virtue of the fact that David Broome was the reigning world champion, having won the title in 1970 at La Baule with Douglas Bunn's Beethoven.

In April of that year Forgie travelled to Hickstead. Not to compete, for he had not been in long and was still unclipped and woolly, but to receive his award from the Irish Horse Board. The magnificent trophy was presented to owner Fred Hartill by Mr. Noel Tanner and the groom received a special prize but there was nothing for the rider. Paddy said jokingly to Irish show jumper Leslie Fitzpatrick, who was standing beside him and is a jeweller, "And what do I get?", to which Leslie replied, "The pleasure of having ridden the horse". But some months later Leslie presented Paddy with a lovely solid silver horse mounted on a plinth and suitably inscribed with the following words, "Presented to Paddy McMahon, the rider of Pennwood Forge Mill". The next British horse to win this award was Heatwave in 1977, who was ridden by David Broome, and it came to Britain again in 1978, going to Sportsman, also ridden by David.

When Forgie started jumping he did not seem to be going quite as well as the previous season, although he was still reaping his fair share of prizes. His connections were very anxious to get selected for the World Championships and the pressure was really on, for Sally at least it was not such a 'fun' sort of year — there was so much at stake.

His first big show was Royal Windsor where he won the final event, the Merck, Sharp and Dohme Supreme Championship, in an eight-horse jump-off to clock 39·3 seconds. Later that month at the Bath and West Show, where more often than not he goes well, he walked away with two of the four main classes. Paddy enjoyed a change of scene here when riding Mrs. Quinney's lovely home-bred Fidelio to win the Working Hunter class.

It had been on the cards for a long time that Paddy and Forge Mill had a good chance of being selected to represent Britain in the World Show Jumping Championships — with their form they could not be ignored. He was duly chosen by the B.S.J.A. selectors, along with David Broome and Harvey Smith. As the host nation we were allowed three riders as against the two of other countries.

Again Forge Mill's itinerary had been carefully planned and it was decided to go to Lucerne as the Americans were taking part and Paddy wanted a chance to compete against them before the World Championships. Forgie travelled to Lucerne on Rowland Fernyhough's lorry, with Valerie Hartill stepping in to act as groom in place of Sally Warren who was ill. She was really put in at the deep end, she hadn't even ridden the horse before. Fortunately she found the other grooms very helpful, in particular Rowland's sister Ailsa (now Mrs. Jones) and Gill, the girl who was doing the Edgars' horses at that time. Somehow she coped but she hadn't realised how much work was involved and there were so many little things to learn. Val's plaiting wasn't very expert so she did a deal with Ailsa that in return for Val doing all the mucking out Ailsa would do all the plaiting!

Paddy also took Pennwood Holvair, formerly called Upton when owned by Jo Daniell (now Mrs. Challens). Upton had done very well in Working Hunter classes and smaller show jumping events when ridden by Jo but he and Paddy never really hit it off. He was also jumped by David Broome and Ray Howe and then passed on to Harvey Smith. Now called Sanyo Video he enjoyed a highly successful 1978 season ridden by Harvey's elder son, Robert. Our other team members in Lucerne were Malcolm Pyrah, Ted Edgar, Rowland Fernyhough, Judy Crago and Lady Frazer. Chef d'Equipe was Col. Guy Wathen, himself a member of the British team there in 1950 riding Strathmore.

The arena is set on the side of Lake Lucerne on blue marl. Normally the going here is very good but when you get a lot of rain, as they did before the 1974 show, it goes like blue clay and the horses were going in six inches. Forge Mill got off to a good start by winning the Preis Bucherer contested over a big track in the heavy going. This was a two-round competition and in the first only three could jump clear, Malcolm Pyrah with Law Court, Gerd Wiltfang with Firlefanz and Judy Crago with Brevitt Bouncer. Pulling hard, Forge Mill ran out at the last fence for three faults. The three clear rounders all got eight faults in the second round and Switzerland's Paul Weir riding Wulf went into the lead with a clear round to add to his first round score of four. Last but one to go, Paddy knew he had to go clear to win. Deciding the best course of action was to take his time and running wide into the double the pair were faultless to record a fine victory for Britain. This was a good show for us as Malcolm Pyrah won a class on April Love and Rowland

71

Fernyhough two on Three Castles.

The Nations Cup took place in extremely severe conditions, the relentless rain barely ceasing until just before the start of the event in this tree-lined arena on the shores of Lake Lucerne. Our team was named as Malcolm Pyrah with Law Court, Rowland Fernyhough with Autumatic, Judy Crago with Brevitt Bouncer and Paddy and Pennwood Forge Mill. Two of these horses were to go on to be in our Olympic squad in Montreal in 1976 but with different riders—Law Court being ridden by Peter Robeson and Bouncer by Rowland Fernyhough.

At the half-way stage we were in front, with 12 faults, of the seven other nations, followed by the Americans on 20½ and the Germans on 24. With a second round clear from Forgie and four faults from Brevitt Bouncer and Law Court we were home (if not dry!) on 20 faults to Germany's 36. Omega invited the British riders to a party afterwards, which was much enjoyed by all. Forgie competing in the Puissance on this deep going pulled a muscle in his neck landing over the big wall. This restricted his movement and he couldn't use himself as freely as normal. This injury was to prove a big factor in the outcome of the World Championships.

Returning to England, he competed in a couple of shows including the Royal where he was fifth in the Texaco and second in the Dunhill. At the following Midlands International he was equal first in the Puissance with four others. But he was never going really freely and veterinary surgeon, the late Richard Hartley, diagnosed torn muscles. For therapy Forgie was sent to Aubrey Langton's equine swimming pool at Bishop's Itchington in Warwickshire.

Horses can often go wrong or be off colour just when you want them at their best, for they are not machines. And so it was that Forgie arrived at Hickstead not at the peak of his fitness with a very sore neck. He was not lame but didn't use himself in his normal way. He wasn't eating well and everything seemed to be going wrong. These problems added to the tensions which were already great with a competition of this sort when the hopes of the country rest on your shoulders.

Sally was back in action by now but Valerie travelled to Hickstead with her to act as general dogsbody, mucking out and carrying the water. She found she learnt a lot by just watching and helping without having the overall responsibility.

The World Championships take place every four years and on this occasion a record entry from 15 different nations had been received. The British trio selected to represent us were the defending champion David Broome, this time with Sportsman, Harvey Smith with Salvador and Paddy McMahon with Pennwood Forge Mill. The competition is staged on a points system with the top four riders over the three legs going forward into the final where they each ride each other's horses. There are many people who criticise this method for they feel top class horses could be ruined. The four who make this final are the best in the world and normally nothing terrible happens with the horses going well and returning to their original form immediately after the championships.

We knew that the courses would be some of the biggest and most difficult since the previous World Championships and amongst the most fancied riders were David Broome, the German pair Hartwig Steenken with his great mare Simona and Alwin Schockemöhle with Rex the Robber. Hubert Parot, the Frenchman who had gone so close in the European Championships, and Nelson Pessoa of Brazil could not be dismissed. Dougie Bunn was determined to put on the best show in the world and the spectacle for the final day was fantastic with the big International arena at Hickstead really lending itself to the occasion.

Course builder was our own Pam Carruthers and the first leg was contested over a 13-fence course which included two doubles, a treble and a number of big square oxers which many of the riders did not like when they walked the course.

This was a speed event with seven seconds added for each fence knocked down. The fences which caused the most trouble were the narrow upright poles (Fence 11) and the first of the twin parallels over the twin water ditches. It was here that Alwin Schockemöhle and Rex the Robber departed from the scene, having been eliminated. Five jumped clear — Hugo Simon for Austria on Lavendel, John Cottle of New Zealand on Rifleman, Eddie Macken of Ireland on Pele, Eddie Cuepper of Belgium on Le Champion and Hartwig Steenken of Germany with Simona.

Sportsman blazed the trail, jumping well, to have the first part of the double down (Fence 3) in 107·8 seconds with seven seconds added for the knock down. He led until a quarter of the riders had been when Simon and Lavendel were the first to go clear in 99·1 seconds. John Cottle, not amongst the fancied riders, went clear in 125·5 seconds before the Irish wizard, Eddie Macken, took Pele into the lead in 95·6 seconds, a position he was to hold until the end of the competition.

Paddy and Forge Mill annoyingly hit one of the smallest fences on the course, the balustrade at Number 6, which eventually put them down to fourth place in 103·1 seconds. Harvey Smith and Salvador had two fences down to finish 11th. At the end of the first day the placings were Eddie Macken, Hugo Simon, Hartwig Steenken, and Paddy McMahon. This order was not to alter after the second leg over eight really imposing Puissance-type fences, which had caused great alarm amongst the riders when they walked the course. But doubts were soon dispelled when Eddie Macken and Pele, first in, went clear, soon to be followed by eight others, including all three British riders, although Forge Mill hit a couple of fences pretty hard. From these eight only Pele and Forge Mill again jumped clear to divide first prize and the equal four-faulters, who took equal third place, were Harvey Smith with Salvador and the American Rodney Jenkins with Idle Dice. Frank Chapot, also of America, was fifth with Main Spring and David Broome sixth on

Sportsman. At the end of the second day the order was Macken 57·75; Simon 55·75; Steenken 54·75; McMahon 53·75; Broome 44; Smith 42; Chapot 42. The chances of at least one British rider getting into the final were high. Paddy had a great chance of winning and the tension was really mounting.

Contested over a Nations Cup-type course of 13 fences the bogey fence in the third leg proved to be Number 13, the final treble. The first part was a vertical brush and rail, the middle a green hurdle oxer and the final part a green bush oxer carrying a spread of two metres. There were few who did not fault here.

Britain's first pair were Harvey Smith and Salvador and they had 12 faults. Sportsman and David Broome were in the 14 ft. 9 in. water and hit the upright before the treble, but were clear at the bogey for eight faults. Steenken and Simona jumped a lovely clear, as did Idle Dice, Lavendel and Pele. The pressure was really on Paddy, he knew he had to finish in the first four in order to qualify for the final. Forge Mill, although bouncing a few poles and looking far from happy, was clear until the final treble but here he ran out of steam, rattling the second element hard before stopping on the way out. They got through the second time but with the first part down to finish on seven faults plus 4¼ time faults. Paddy's chance had gone.

In the second round only Steenken and Simona could achieve a double clear, Pele and Lavendel both having four faults to dispute second place. Forge Mill was out of the reckoning with three fences down in the second round and the coveted fourth place for the final rested between David Broome and Frank Chapot. Sportsman had the fence down going into the treble to make a total of 12, whilst Main Spring also had one down for a total of eight and went forward to the final. Paddy had been in with such a good chance, he had come so near and yet so far from the world title, but that's the luck of the game. They finished in sixth place overall.

The bands of four regiments of Guards accompanied the four finalists into the arena. The atmosphere was electric, the stands were packed to bursting and spectators were thick along the rails. The course of eight fences was, as was to be expected, less demanding than those for the three qualifying competitions but still severe enough when riding a completely strange horse after only a three-minute riding-in period. All four were clear on their own horses and after riding each other's Steenken and Macken were level on four faults with Simon and Chapot but one fence away on eight. Going first in the jump-off Eddie Macken and Pele had the oxer down and then speeding on a bit were in the water for eight faults in 45·6 seconds. In a never-to-be-forgotten round Steenken and his lovely 16-year-old Hanoverian mare Simona were in the water, but otherwise faultless to clinch the world title. A well-deserved victory for a great rider and a mare whose like we will be fortunate to see again, she was brilliant. Tragically, Hartwig was to die in 1976, following a road accident from which he never regained consciousness. Ironically, Eddie Macken was to go on to miss a second world title in 1978 at Aachen when he finished second to another German, this time beaten by the clock (he incurred a quarter time fault riding Pandur II) and Gerd Wiltfang.

It was during the World Championships at Hickstead that Sally Warren told Fred Hartill that regretfully she had decided to leave. She was very sad to go after years of sharing the ups and down of this great horse, who is as honest as the day is long.

Her last show was the Royal International at Wembley and, unfortunately, this was a bad week for the Pennwood contingent as Forgie was obviously feeling the effects of the gruelling World Championships and did not go well. It was a pity that she couldn't end her association with Forge Mill on a high note for she had shared so many big occasions but you can't be on the crest of a wave for ever and horses are great levellers. Sally, an attractive and charming blonde, is now living in Shropshire where she runs a dealing yard.

Valerie Hartill had been helping Sally with the horses for the past few weeks so the change-over went very smoothly when she took over the reins immediately following the International. Forgie was, however, sent away for three weeks to Richard Hartley's veterinary establishment in Hampshire to receive treatment for his torn muscles which were still causing problems. He therefore missed the Professional/Amateur Championships at Cardiff Castle in July. These important championships are held in a delightful setting with the towering walls of the castle acting as a backcloth and peacocks strutting around and even in the ring. This was Valerie's first show with Paddy since she took over completely and they took Streamline and Fanta, both owned by Mr. Conway at the time.

Forgie was back in action for the August Hickstead meeting, finishing second in the Castella Stakes to Malcolm Pyrah and Trevarrion after a six-cornered jump-off. In the Derby trial he knocked up 23 faults and in the Derby itself was lucky to escape without a fall at the big privet oxer and totalled 16 faults. The winner for the third time was Harvey Smith, this time riding Salvador, a horse he bought from Alwin Schockemöhle.

After Hickstead came Southport, where he went better to win a big class. They rose early the following morning, plaited by torchlight and set off at crack of dawn for the British Timken Show in Northamptonshire. Arriving just as everybody was sitting down to breakfast, they discovered that their class was not in the morning, as Paddy had thought, but at 2 p.m., the early start had been unnecessary. Valerie wasn't best pleased but was restored to good humour when Forgie performed brilliantly to take second place in the Olympic Trial behind Graham Fletcher and Buttevant Boy, runners-up in the British Jumping Derby six days earlier. Forge Mill has, in fact, a very good record in this event which is always decided, as its name implies, over a big Olympic-type course.

The B.S.J.A. National Championship took place at

Hickstead that year, Forgie being one of five horses clear over Pam Carruthers' track. The only one who could repeat this performance was young Pip Nicholls riding Timmie who at only 17 must be the youngest winner ever. Paddy also qualified Fanta for the final, finishing third on him and fourth on Forge Mill.

As preparation for jumping indoors Forgie competed at the Everest Double Glazing Championships at Stoneleigh and also at Allerton. Here he won a class on the opening day but on the second slipped and pulled a leg muscle. The late Mr. Dawes, a local vet from West Bromwich, decided the best thing to do was to blister him and turn him away for the rest of the season. He told Fred Hartill that he could possibly get him right but he was not just *any* horse and if they wanted to get more jumping out of him they would be wise to rest him for a while. Mr. Dawes was a great fan of Forgie and considered him a great horse, the like of which you don't find every day.

The familiar face of Pennwood Forge Mill was therefore sadly missing from the Horse of the Year Show and the Olympia Christmas Show. The year which had started so well had ended on a bad note.

10

"TRAVEL GALORE"

1975 was European Championship year once more but Paddy as a professional would not be able to take part for they were open only to amateurs. At the start of the season Forgie accompanied the rest of the Pennwood team to Amberley and Lincoln Shows, not to compete, for he was still very woolly, but to be exercised. Paddy was a great believer in swimming horses and Forgie spent many hours in Aubrey Langton's pool near Southam. Newark and Notts Show at the beginning of May was first on the agenda, followed by Thorsesby where, despite a bandage coming undone, he finished fourth in the Open. A long journey to Devon County followed, his travelling companions being Fanta and Streamline, and was rewarded with a second place in the Radio Rentals A.I.T. behind Harvey Smith and Salvador, beaten by two seconds.

The Shropshire and West Midland Show heralded the start of a long absence from home for Paddy, Valerie, Forgie, Streamline and Fanta. Next was Royal Windsor where the ground was rock hard, so Forgie only jumped on the first day. Valerie well remembers this show for Fanta stamped on her foot making it painfully sore. It had to be strapped up with Valerie hobbling around. Surrey County Show at Guildford reaped a third prize for Forgie before going on to the Bath and West Show where he was placed each day, tying for first place on the opening day with Caroline Bradley and Acrobat. Paddy won the Radio Rentals Stakes here with Streamline.

The intention was to go on to the Butlins Show at Pwllheli in Wales from here but Paddy was feeling rather ill the following morning (as were some of the other riders for there had been a party!) so they didn't go. Instead the horses went to Brian Dye's house for a couple of nights prior to the South of England Show. The house is in the direct flight path for Gatwick Airport and for the first hour Forgie ducked every time a plane went over his stable! At Ardingly the ground was again very hard but Forgie, in devastating form, won the big class on the first day and the A.I.T. on the last, having been rested on the middle day.

Home was a welcome sight after nearly three weeks away, especially for poor Valerie who was still very lame. An X-ray revealed she had, in fact, broken a bone in her foot when Fanta trod on her but having been strapped up so tightly it was mending itself. The respite at Pennwood was, however, brief, for three days later it was off to Wales for the popular Cardiff Pro/Am Championships. Forgie finished second in the second leg to Eddie Macken and Boomerang and fourth overall in the Professional Championship won by Stephen Hadley on Corunna Bay.

From Cardiff it was straight to Fontainebleau, travelling with the Fernyhoughs from Newhaven and arriving at around 2 a.m. amid pouring rain. At the front were some beautiful stables but the show jumpers were directed to some less smart ones in a backyard where there were no lights and straw was stacked up so high around the doors you couldn't get in. By the time they had moved the straw, put the beds down and settled their charges it was 4 a.m. and it was some very weary grooms who tumbled thankfully into bed. The showground is a 20-minute drive away and, although in a lovely setting, lacks atmosphere for there were no spectators, even for the big events. The courses were galloping tracks with small fences which did not altogether suit a horse of Forge Mill's calibre. For instance, he jumped two clear rounds in the Grand Prix but only finished ninth on time, the others just galloped round flat out, getting away with it over these small fences.

In the Puissance the going was very sticky and Forgie was withdrawn from the final round to stand third. The Nations Cup course, by contrast, was big and demanding in the wet ground. This was a bad Cup for Britain who could finish no higher than fifth. In the first round Paddy had a fence down and then missed one, luckily realising and going back to jump it within the time allowed and in the second round had four faults. Also in our team was the promising Arksey, then ridden by Tim Grubb. Arksey was to join the Pennwood stable in August 1978 to travel with Forgie as Geoff Glazzard's second string. In fact, Fontainebleau was a bad show for Britain for we came away without even one first prize.

On the Monday morning the rest of the team travelled on to Aachen but Forgie returned home for another Royal Show. This is Britain's largest agricultural show, attended by nearly a quarter of a million people over the four days. Show jumping is always a popular part of the Grand Ring programme at Stoneleigh. Forgie won the Hennessy Trophy and was third in the Texaco Championship, a competition he'd won twice before. The East of England Show at Peterborough brought another Hennessy win, his second in less than three weeks — it's fortunate that Fred Hartill is partial to a drop of brandy!

In 1975 official recognition was given for the Prince of Wales Cup to be staged at Hickstead as an official Nations Cup. When the team was announced it included Paddy and Pennwood Forge Mill, along with David Broome, Harvey Smith and Graham Fletcher. Against strong opposition the home side of Paddy and Forge Mill, David with Heatwave, Harvey riding Salvador and Graham with Tauna Dora ran out the winners by eight faults to Germany's nine, a very close finish. Ronnie Masserella, the team captain, had moulded together a great team that could take on and beat the best in the world.

The following week's Royal International saw the tragic accident to another horse of enormous scope, the chesnut Beau Supreme, ridden by Derek Ricketts. During the first round of the King George V Gold Cup he broke his off-foreleg and had to be destroyed. Next into the arena were Paddy and Forge Mill and the horse was reluctant to go past the corpse of poor Beau Supreme on the sledge in the collecting ring and Paddy and the other riders were shaken by the tragedy. Forgie eventually finished third, having jumped a clear round and then had four faults in the jump-off. Popular winner was the handsome Alwin Schockemöhle on Rex the Robber from his great friend and rival David Broome on the American-bred Philco.

For Friday's Daily Mail Cup, Alan Ball built a big combination down the middle of the arena. Paddy was clear to here and galloped down to it a shade too fast with the result that Forgie stopped and dropped him fair and square in the middle.

A regular member of the first squad, Paddy and Pennwood Forge Mill travelled next to Dublin, along with Streamline. On the first day Forgie had one fence down and was third, beaten on time, on the second and third again in the concluding Grand Prix of Ireland. The night before the much sought after Aga Khan Trophy (Nations Cup) Forgie got cast in his box and Valerie was worried in case he had injured himself and couldn't take part. But all was well for he achieved a four fault round (at the second fence) in the first round and a splendid clear in the second to help clinch the trophy for Britain for the third time, thus making it our outright property. Our other winning team members were Harvey Smith with Salvador, 8 and 4; Graham Fletcher and

Tauna Dora, 4 and 4; and David Broome and Heatwave, 0 and no second round. With 16 faults we finished 13 faults ahead of Ireland with West Germany third. We had recorded a fine double with the Prince of Wales Cup at Hickstead and now the Aga Khan Trophy in Dublin with the same team.

It rained heavily throughout the Hickstead August meeting making conditions treacherous. Forgie was second in the Derby Trial to Eddie Macken with Boomerang, with Eddie going on to win the Derby itself on the Sunday with Pele. No horse which has won the trial has ever gone on to win the actual Derby in the same year. Forge Mill finished equal eighth.

Bags packed once more it was off to Rotterdam some ten days later, travelling with Freddie Broome. What had started as a hard dry summer had by now developed into a decidedly wet one and here too it poured with rain for much of the show. Stabled as they were in tents didn't suit Forge Mill so he ripped the top out of his so that he could look out and get some fresh air. The result was that Forgie and bedding were soon soaking and a quick repair job had to be done. Here we finished second in the Nations Cup to Germany, thus clinching the President's Trophy for the third time, with Forge Mill jumping a double clear round. The President's Trophy was presented in 1965 by Prince Philip and goes to the country gaining the most number of points in Nations Cups throughout the season.

Organised by the Broome family at their Mount Ballan Manor home near Chepstow the Wales and West Show is based on a smaller version of Hickstead having as it does permanent obstacles such as a Bank, Table and Devil's Dyke. Then it was off abroad again this time to St. Gallen in Switzerland spending a night at Fontainbleau en route. Once more the stabling was of a very temporary nature with rather flimsy bars dividing the horses and it was here that Forgie, forever thinking of his tummy, broke down the rail to get at Streamline's hay, having already eaten his own!

Fanta fell heavily on Paddy putting him out of action for part of the show.

The much travelled contingent then caught the ferry across Lake Constance to the Salzburg Show and then on to Donaueschingen. At this show the Leading Rider was to be presented with a car and the Pennwood team had been boasting that they would be returning to Wolverhampton with it. It was therefore a rather crestfallen Paddy who returned not with the car but a push-bike for a minor placing down the line! The entries in each class were very big here and once more the weather was bad, with terrific thunderstorms. During one of these the other grooms and horses dashed for the shelter of the trees but Forgie refused to go under them (perfectly sensibly) preferring to stand in the torrential rain. As a result both he and Valerie looked like drowned rats!

Stabling at Aachen on the return trip they were late leaving and missed the vet at the border so didn't get their papers stamped. On arriving in England they were told that as their papers weren't in order they would have to go into quarantine for three weeks. So they went back to the Broome's home feeling very worried, for it would mean missing the Horse of the Year Show. But eventually things were sorted out and they were allowed out of isolation before the three weeks were up.

Forgie embarked on another swimming campaign prior to the Everest Double Glazing Championships at Stoneleigh. Here, over an enormous course, he won the Everest Double Glazing Championship putting up a marvellous performance to beat Sportsman and David Broome in the final. Back at Wembley he finished second on the final night in the Radio Rentals Championship to Eddie Macken and Boomerang.

A short and well deserved rest period followed before the Amsterdam Show where he won the opening class. At this Dutch Show they don't start jumping until about 5 p.m. and consequently don't finish until very late at night. Fanta went well at Amsterdam and then made the journey to Berlin with Streamline. Valerie stayed at home with Forgie as Pauline Cushing (Derek Rickett's former groom) was doing Paddy's horses as she wanted a trip to Germany in order to work out there. From here Paddy was to go on to Brussels with Valerie travelling out with the Johnseys to join him.

A few days before she was due to leave she received a telephone call from Paddy asking her to bring Forge Mill out. So Valerie had to hastily beg the Johnseys to take Forge Mill in addition to herself and set to clipping the horse and getting his papers in order. He was looking very woolly as he was being exercised each day and turned out at night in his New Zealand rug. It was in Brussels that Forge Mill competed in his last Puissance. He jumped the big wall at 7ft. 3 in. but at the next attempt (7 ft. 5 in.) the horse wouldn't go anywhere near it, just standing at the bottom of the arena refusing to move. So Paddy had no alternative but to retire him into third place. As there was nowhere to eat on the showground the English grooms decided to find somewhere in town. On their return they were horrified to find that the gates had been locked so they couldn't get back in. Most of the party managed to squeeze through some turnstiles but some had to find other means and eventually got in by climbing over a big wall.

Returning home, on Saturday 13th December Forge Mill performed the opening ceremony at the Cosford Saddle Club Indoor Arena some seven miles from Wolverhampton in the Newport direction. This club caters mainly for R.A.F. staff. So to Christmas and the fairy tale atmosphere of Olympia where he was placed in most of the classes despite having 'four-faultitis' again.

For the 1976 season Valerie had one or two promising novices to jump, such as Cottage Gold a mare out of Pennwood Gold Flake by Marine Corps. She was only small but had ability if only she would put her mind to it, which most of the time she didn't! She was a little devil with a mind of her own, it was no use telling her what to do. She went on to be ridden by Geoff Glazzard who did well on her during the winter before she was sold to Denmark.

As Valerie was busy jumping the novices, Forge Mill was looked after during the 1976 season by a variety of girls who worked at Pennwood. It was another busy year for Forge Mill because he and Paddy travelled to a lot of shows. They made their debut a winning one at the South Western Show and then went on to Doncaster where they won the Championship at the Pageant of the Horse. Yet another Area International Trial came to them in May at the Shropshire and West Midlands and at Burley-on-the-Hill they won the Speed and Puissance events.

It was in May 1976 that Paddy married former air hostess Patricia Cox at Stratford-on-Avon with Forge Mill as guest of honour. At the Bath and West they won the Cockburn Special Reserve Stakes and placings followed in A.I.T.'s at Three Counties and Royal Norfolk, where he also shared first place in the Holden Motors Stakes with David Broome. At the Cardiff Pro/Am Championships he was sixth in the first leg, ninth in the second and 11th in the third. It was at Cardiff that he experienced a fall which made him extra careful for the following Royal Show. Here he won the Texaco Trophy for the third time and on the final day in the Radio Rentals Grand Prix he made another awkward jump. He took a short one to the wall of a double and deciding that discretion is the better part of valour slipped out the side door at the second element. At the Northampton Show he won yet another Area International Trial before going on to the Royal International. On the first day he came past the entrance and approached the first fence down the side of the arena. He was on a long stride, met it too far back and stopped. In fact he did no good at this show at all, which is very unusual for him as he loves Wembley and the proximity of the crowd.

Then up to Lancashire for the Bass Lancs Show where he was placed in several classes before another tilt at the British Jumping Derby. The course constructed for the Derby Trial caused a 'demo' led by some of our leading professional riders who thought the course was too big. Their pleas were listened to and subsequently the track lowered on the instructions of Douglas Bunn. Paddy and Pennwood Forge Mill had an annoying four faults at the very first fence, to finish equal second with seven others. The only clear round came from Rowland Fernyhough and Autumatic. The Derby itself resulted in a second win in this show jumping classic for the golden boy of Irish jumping, Eddie Macken, this time with Boomerang. Forge Mill finished equal twelfth.

With winter approaching once more it was back to the indoor shows with a win at Mill Lodge and placings at the Everest Double Glazing Championships at Stoneleigh. At the Horse of the Year Show their only placing was a fifth in the Sunday Times Cup. Forge Mill seemed to be losing some of his form and consistency.

Forgie had his break at this time of year and then it was off to Amsterdam in Holland. On their return Christmas was drawing near and it was time for Olympia where Forge Mill did not go particularly well, although he did finish second in one competition. There were many people in the show jumping world who said the horse was finished. He had been a grand warrior but they thought the spark had gone. He was getting into trouble in combination fences and stopping on a number of occasions. He had been at the very top of the show jumping tree for five years and had done a great deal during this time. Nevertheless, he headed the list of National Prizewinners and finished sixth in the Combined list for home and International winners.

11

LIFE BEHIND THE SCENES

Many people forget that behind the glamorous facade of the
show jumping world there are the grooms who watch and
wait as their beloved charges compete. They put in hours of
hard work, very often with an early start and late finish and
lots of travelling between shows. Sometimes there are long
and boring waits between classes. It is up to the grooms to
feed and exercise the horses correctly so that they are at the
peak of their fitness for major events. At times they have to
put up with very makeshift conditions for their horses
especially when travelling abroad and carry a lot of
responsibility. However, for the majority of them it is all
worthwhile, the joy of seeing their horses go well is reward
enough.

Sally Warren was Forgie's devoted groom for just over
three years, from 1971 until the middle of the 1974 season
when her successor was Fred Hartill's daughter, Valerie,
then aged 18, who still does Forgie.

Always pony mad Sally started riding at the age of three.
She remembers that her first show was Richmond Royal
Horse Show where, riding a pony called Kim, she won a

special prize for being the youngest competitor. She went through the usual rigours of the Pony Club being a keen member of the Old Surrey and Burstow Branch. From the age of eight until she was 13 she rode show ponies but her one ambition was to jump so the 13.2 h.h. Dandino V was purchased for her. From him she progressed on to the bigger Oliver Twist for B.S.J.A. Affiliated shows.

On leaving school Sally took a job with the Harries family in Sussex working with Eric Jones. Amongst the horses in the yard were Manhattan (which David Broome took to the 1972 Olympics in Munich), a horse formerly known as Flair, which I used to have and one Sally used to jump called Golden Springs.

Sally's father was rather against her working with horses and thought she ought to go into the hotel trade as a trainee receptionist and this she did. However, she still yearned for the horses and when offered a summer job by Brazilian ace Nelson Pessoa leapt at the chance. Nelson, one of the greatest show jumpers in the world, is based in France. During the time spent with him Sally went to the Men's World Championships at La Baule, won by David Broome riding Beethoven.

On returning to England, instead of going back into the hotel trade she joined Trevor Banks' stable in Yorkshire, travelling all the major shows at home and abroad with the British team when doing Mike Saywell's horses. It was in 1971 that she came to Pennwood, about two months after Forge Mill returned to the yard from John Wrathall. She met Fred Hartill at Royal Windsor and was offered the job. As soon as she saw Forge Mill and Paddy in action she thought, "Oh, yes, this is a good horse", and took the job.

Strangely enough, and illustrating what a small world it is, some years previously Sally had gone for an interview with a farmer in Northamptonshire after seeing his advertisement in 'Horse and Hound'. She was shown around the stables and in one box was a big horse with an ugly head. The man said, "I've only had him a couple of days but one day he'll be a great horse". The name of the person was John Wrathall and the horse Pennwood Forge Mill! Sally didn't go to work for the Wrathalls but fate was to dictate that her path and Forgie's should cross a few years later.

It was a bit of a gamble for Sally when she came to Pennwood, for she had gained a taste for travelling with Trevor Banks' string. At that time there was nothing but hope and ambition to suggest that Forge Mill would make the grade as an International horse and Sally would get the chance to continue her travels abroad which she enjoyed so much.

Sally told me of some of the more amusing incidents which took place during the time she spent with Forgie. One day at the Christmas Olympia Show Sally left him eating his supper with the door ajar for she knew he wouldn't move away from his food, while she just popped around the corner for a few minutes. On her return she was horrified to find the horse gone. Then she heard laughter and saw the late Hartwig Steenken and his groom grinning all over their faces. They had seen her go and had quickly whipped in and removed Forge Mill from his box and hidden him around the corner. He was looking very disgruntled at being taken away from his food!

One day at Hickstead Forge Mill and Paddy were doing some advertising. It was all taking rather a long time so Paddy decided to go off for a meal. The camera crew meanwhile asked Sally if she would canter the horse around the vast Hickstead arena so that they could get the sound right. It was, she told me, an incredible feeling. She had, of course, ridden him at home but it was a very different matter here for he felt so strong and thought he was in there to jump as usual. She felt quite panicky in case she couldn't stop.

On another occasion, again at Hickstead, Sally decided to take him in the Conformation Class which precedes the Jumping Derby. This caused great amusement amongst the other grooms for Forgie would never win a show class. But handsome is as handsome does and Forge Mill has proved time and time again that you don't have to be beautiful to beat the best in the world. Once, when travelling the Continental shows, the back of the box became rather dirty and the foreign grooms, for a joke, wrote on the back, "Forge Mill for Sale". Sally was at a loss to understand why so many people were coming up trying to buy the horse until suddenly she saw the notice on the back of the lorry!

One of the French riders was in the prize money at the Madrid Show and, as his groom had taken his horse back to the stables, he asked if he could ride Forge Mill into the ring to collect his rosette. Coming out, he remarked that he was the most impressive horse he'd ever ridden, there was so much impulsion there, you just have to touch him with your legs and he's gone. So totally different to the impression he gives as he saunters into the ring looking completely unperturbed and half asleep. When Sally was at Pennwood, one of his favourite tricks was taking sugar lumps and carrots out of her mouth, pawing the ground first to say please.

A typical non-show day in the life of Pennwood Forge Mill starts at 7.30 a.m. with his morning feed. As soon as he sees Valerie approaching he starts banging his door, but he doesn't do it when other people pass. He has another feed at night but not one at midday as they feel that if you give him one at home he will also expect it at a show when he is jumping and can't have it. They therefore make the other two feeds bigger in consequence. His diet has, in fact, always been a problem as Forgie has to watch his weight, being inclined to chubbiness. Being a big horse he needs all the protein he can get and to warrant all the hard food he needs roughage but big haynets are out of the question as they blow him out like a barrel.

Now for his eating habits. He's a messy feeder and likes to upset his feed into his shavings and then pick it out. Sometimes he gets competition for his food from the birds which fly into his stable and this makes him wild. In fact, he doesn't really like anybody in his box, it's his domain and he chases dogs who are bold enough to enter. The black and white cat, Timmy, as a kitten used to go into his stable and sit on the rafters, occasionally being brave enough to venture down on to his back. Forgie would get very cross and try to nip the kitten's tail as it played on the rafters.

Grooming takes up roughly an hour each day. Forgie is rather a dirty horse and doesn't really like being brushed. He thinks it's funny to get dirty again when he's just been strapped and digs in his shavings to create dust. He will grind his teeth and lash out with his hind legs but really it's all in fun because he's feeling so well and full of beans. He loves rubbing his plaits out, so has to be tied up when this has been done at a show, but he still always manages to rub his tail.

Forgie is given half an hour's flat work each day which bores him terribly. Valerie finds that her methods have to be totally different from those you would use with most horses so she always gallops him first to give him a pipe opener and a chance to let off steam as she finds this settles him. He is very strong for the first 10 to 15 minutes when he does his flat work before either going for a hack or up and down the steep banks surrounding the house. These are ideal for toning up his jumping muscles and he thinks it's all great fun. He gets at least an hour's work per day.

One of his favourite pastimes is to be taken for a ride through the woods, jumping the small logs he encounters along the route. They are so minute compared with the big fences he faces in the ring but it gives him so much pleasure. Some days he is boxed to Baggeridge Woods, a former colliery where you can ride for 20 or 30 miles along the disused railway line. Valerie feels that now he is older this is more beneficial to him than a lot of work on the flat for it makes him more relaxed.

Exercising around the roads of Penn always takes a long time, especially if Forgie is wearing his rug with his name on it. All the people they meet stop to admire him and have a chat and ask, "Is it really *him*?". He gets very spoilt with lots of apples, carrots and sugar. The golfers on Penn Common often pause in their strokes to look at the local hero as he passes. He enjoys all the attention for he loves people and he's super in traffic.

At the beginning of the season Valerie jumps him over small fences to get him going but once the season is under way he is rarely jumped at home. Nor does Geoff ride him between shows. This is probably a good thing for it means that he has a certain edge when he does ride him at a show.

Forgie is turned out each day for an hour, very often with the tiny piebald pony Magpie whom he clearly adores. Magpie is aged 39 and returns the affection although he squeals madly each time Forgie nestles him. During Forgie's winter rest the pair are turned out together each day but it's not encouraged too much in the summer as it is easy for a horse to become too dependent on a companion and not want to leave him to go to shows.

On the way out to his special paddock Forgie has to collect his apple from Mrs. Hartill at the back door. He is very particular, showing a preference for Granny Smiths, and he also likes oranges. Arksey, who was Forgie's travelling companion for part of the 1978 season, soon caught this habit and even tried to get his enormous frame through the back door! To reach the paddock you have to cross Pennwood Lane and here Forgie looks both ways before crossing. One day when being unloaded late at night from a show he escaped and headed off towards the paddock. However, when nobody came looking for him he just turned round and trotted back up the lane towards them. When he's turned out he likes to be waited on and expects Mrs. Cook, who lives in the house bordering his paddock, to get him a bucket of water to drink from if she's at home. If not, he will drink quite happily from the trough! He's very good to catch, you only have to call him and he comes. When Paddy was there his Jack Russell, Mandy (now dead), would often lead him in from the field. Sally Warren still has

94

Mandy's son which she called Dikler, after his father who belonged to Olympic rider Rowland Fernyhough.

One of Forgie's main hates is being clipped and having his whiskers cut. As soon as you enter his box with the clippers, even if they're hidden, he knows and starts groaning loudly. Nowadays they dope him to clip him but still have to use a twitch to do his head. If a casual visitor came into the yard and heard his groans they'd think a murder was being committed!

Another thing he doesn't like are camels. At Olympia when the camels are appearing he won't go out of his stable when they are around. Nor, like a lot of horses, does he like pigs, but elephants don't bother him at all. He loves donkeys and small ponies and at the last Horse of the Year Show was fascinated by one of the small ponies taking part in the Personality Parade and kept following it around the collecting ring.

Ice cream and lollies also number amongst his likes as do chocolates, which his fans send him by the box-full. He has his preferences, though, and only picks out certain varieties such as soft centres and toffees, ignoring the other types. He shows a definite preference for milk chocolates rather than plain!

He has always been funny about his head being touched and some days can be very difficult. He's hard to plait on these occasions but funnily enough these are the days he jumps best, when he's edgy and spooky. If he's at a show such as Wembley or Olympia in the middle of London and can't get his daily grass, he doesn't like it all and often his jumping goes off as the week progresses. Being able to turn a horse out each day, even for ten minutes, relieves the tension and relaxes them. I am a great believer in it.

Forgie has good feet although they're on the small side for a horse of his size. With him being on shavings they tend to be rather brittle so they have to try to keep them soft. During Sally's days somebody suggested a good remedy was to put them in cow dung, so she had to get plastic sacks full of smelly cow dung and stick his feet in them for hours. Slightly nicer methods and certainly less smelly are putting cod liver oil on, which really soaks in, and standing his feet in his own specially made water box. His regular blacksmith Neville Smith told me, "He's very good to shoe and would try to help you if he could. Over all the years I've done him I've never known him kick although he does occasionally have a little nip, but only in fun". Neville is very interested in show jumping and has a horse of his own called Farrier's Lad which is ridden by one of his apprentices, Joe Murphy. Neville often bumps into Forge Mill at shows and watches him on television whenever he can. Neville's shoeing gains praise from other blacksmiths all over the country and he was National Shoeing Champion in 1963/4/5. Some of Forgie's shoes have been plated and one was mounted on a trophy presented at the Channel Islands Show a few years back.

Forgie loves children and on one occasion recently Valerie took him to parade at nearby Penn Common Show. The crowd loved him and he enjoyed all the attention and being surrounded and patted by all the local children. He's not too keen on people in his box and one day at Hickstead Paddy decided to mount him in the box. He bucked and bucked until Paddy landed on the floor!

On returning to Penn from shows he always knows when he's nearing home and bangs the floor of the lorry as it rounds the bend at Penn Church. Forgie is happy to be home although he loves exploring new places and must always have a look round before he settles down for the night.

Forge Mill is highly popular with the foreign grooms and with the riders who will go out of their way to come over and pat him, an unusual occurrence in the tough world of show jumping where there is little room for sentiment. They all have enormous respect for the horse.

Forgie looks an absolute picture of health and happiness. He is a great credit to Valerie with his coat gleaming. Forgie has been the star of Pennwood for so long that he was a bit put out when Arksey arrived and got some of the limelight. He sulked for days at first but slowly came to accept him.

The special grooms' prizes which are becoming popular are to be encouraged for the poor hard-working grooms behind the scenes. They need an incentive, getting all the hard work and none of the glory. So good is Valerie's stable care and turn-out that at the 1978 Horse of the Year Show she won the special prize presented to the groom of the best turned-out horse, the judge being leading trainer Dick Stillwell.

She was also second at the 1978 Royal International Horse Show and third at the Wales and West. A fit horse which feels well is a happy, relaxed and contented one.

Valerie started riding at the age of three on Forgie's friend, Magpie, who was bought as a birthday present for her but sometimes used in the riding school. Mind you, he wasn't very popular there as he was such a terror to the little children. Valerie used to accompany her father and Pennwood Gold Flake to local shows with Magpie, just riding round outside. She didn't take to jumping at first but did have a couple of 13.2 h.h. ponies to jump before graduating to Black Gold and Pennwood Pepperpot (not to be confused with Gill Kelly's Pepperpot who is bigger) for 14.2 h.h. classes.

It was when she went up the ladder to horses that she really began to go well, her most successful mount being Kilbrin which she kept for a record two-and-a-half seasons. Valerie enjoys the satisfaction of producing novices and getting them going. She'd like to be able to keep some but knows the Pennwood rules! A nice mare she jumped last winter was Denby (stable name Agnes), a five-year-old for which she has great hopes.

From June until October Valerie is too busy looking after Forge Mill to jump in the ring herself but she competes regularly on an assortment of mounts from October to June. She would like to do more jumping herself as she misses it in many ways but would never give up looking after Forge Mill for she'd hate the thought of anybody else doing him now. Her competitive instincts will have to wait until he retires.

I asked Valerie if she had any ambition to ride Forge Mill in the ring but she told me there would be too much to live up to und anyway the fences were too big and she wasn't very brave! She would rather ride a novice, for then nobody could say she was not riding him as well as the last person. She would, however, like an old Grade 'A' to teach her the tricks of the trade. At Mill Lodge early in the 1978 season she took Forge Mill along just to keep him exercised as she was jumping other horses and Geoff was away. Everybody kept rushing to the ringside when the open classes were in progress expecting to see Valerie making her debut on Pennwood Forge Mill.

At the end of each season Forgie goes to visit the well-known horse vet Peter Thorne at his Radway surgery. Here he is given a thorough check-up and X-rayed to make sure that all is well. He's not too keen on their white coats and on the second day needs a lot of persuasion to get him back into the surgery — it costs the assistants a fortune in 'Polos'. For it is 'Polos' which are his favourite titbit, he has one when he's jumped the practice fence at a show and another after he's completed each round — it's quite a ritual.

Forge Mill has so much energy as was shown when he first arrived at Pennwood and it all has to be used up somehow. He now channels it into his naughty little ways which go towards making him the great character he is. With horses, dogs and a lot of other animals it is their owners and handlers who bring out the best or the worst in them and allow them to develop their individual characters. Forge Mill has been fortunate in having Sally and Valerie to develop his to the full for he has received great love and affection from both. They in return will tell you that they count themselves lucky to have contributed to the success story of this great horse.

Pennwood Forge Mill, the name gives an impression of

calmness and indeed he looks calm as he enters the ring but as you can tell from this chapter he's got lots of naughty habits and odd ways, he can be very moody and varies from day to day. He's got a suspicious nature and many odd quirks and is bang full of character.

When attending a show Valerie will be in action a good two hours before the start of Forgie's class. He has to have his mane plaited, his coat brushed until it shines, his feet oiled and his bandages put on. An hour before he is due to jump Valerie tacks him up and takes him out of the stable, walking him round for an hour to loosen up. About 12 horses before he is due to jump Geoff Glazzard will take over and, after riding him round for a few minutes, pop him over a small practice fence a couple of times, with the reward of a 'Polo' afterwards. As he waits to enter the arena Pennwood Forge Mill stands patiently in the collecting ring, the wise old face saying, "I've done it all before and know just what it's all about".

12

FORGIE TAKES GEOFF TO THE TOP

It was in February 1977 that Paddy announced that he was leaving Pennwood as he and Trish had decided to set up their own yard at Fringford, some four miles out of Bicester in Oxfordshire. He asked to take Forge Mill with him but the Hartills felt they would rather retire him than let him out of the yard. He was such a family pet and part of the Pennwood trademark. Paddy was naturally very upset at this decision and set about building a new string of jumpers to travel the shows.

Paddy and Trish, plus her daughter Nicola (aged 12) from a previous marriage and Paddy's daughter Liz (15), also from a previous marriage, live in a lovely beamed house surrounded by 30 acres. They had to re-build the yard which has stabling for a dozen horses but there was little to do to the house. Paddy also has a son Peter and another daughter called Tricia who lives with her mother. Nicola and Liz attend Wistonbirt Boarding School in Gloucestershire and although they both enjoy riding rarely compete at shows.

The Australian-bred Gollanite Hoescht is Paddy's top

horse at present and he thinks very highly of him. He has a good second string in Mr. and Mrs. Napolitano's Stream-line. He first rode this chesnut in 1974/75 seasons when owned by Mr. Conway and stabled at Pennwood. The ride then went to Marion Mould but she had a bad fall from him at Badminton in 1976 and he was turned out for the rest of the season. Paddy then bought him from Mr. Conway in 1977 and sold him to his present owners. Paddy also has some good novices to bring on.

Although at first set on retiring Pennwood Forge Mill, when the Hartills had given the matter more thought, they decided it would be wrong to retire him for he was still only 13 which is comparatively young for a show jumper. There should be a few more years jumping left in him yet. Fred Hartill toyed with the idea of sending him to one of the top riders but felt that people would associate winning with the rider's ability and not the horse's.

Geoff Glazzard had been riding young horses for Fred Hartill for the past four years and Fred decided he'd like to give the young rider a few outings on Forgie to give him the experience of a really top class horse. The pressure would not be on Forge Mill but on Geoff following in the footsteps of such a successful rider as Paddy McMahon. It would not be easy for him as he would have a lot to live up to and there would be many people only too ready to say the horse was not going as well for him and compare his style of riding with Paddy McMahon's.

In a very short time Pennwood Forge Mill proved he was far from a 'has been' and Geoff Glazzard seized his opportunity with both hands and, rising to the occasion, showed that he could take on and beat the best in the country. He justified Fred Hartill's faith in his ability for there were many who said he was the wrong man for the job and too inexperienced. If I'm honest I have to admit that I was one of them — the doubting Thomases or Sues had been silenced!

Born in 1949 Geoff has always resided around the

Wolverhampton area, now living at Codsall. However, his 18-box yard is at Black Ladies Farm, Brewood, some seven miles from Wolverhampton in the direction of Stafford. Here is based his string of jumpers owned by many different people but always including two or three novices from Pennwood. He moved to Brewood from his original yard at Codsall which he started in 1970 as a livery and riding stables.

From about the age of six Geoff was a regular visitor to his local riding school — this was not Pennwood for he thought it too big and, anyway, the man who ran it frightened him! When he was ten he started going to gymkhanas and it was his practice in these events which helped him get his balance and his eye in. He also did a lot of bare-back riding on a variety of ponies, again a sound basis from which to develop a good deep seat.

Geoff didn't jump ponies, preferring to stick to gymkhanas and in fact only came on to the show jumping scene comparatively late in life, first competing at B.S.J.A. affiliated shows ten years ago. In 1969 he experienced his first taste of the Horse of the Year Show at Wembley when he qualified Buccaneer XXI for the Foxhunter Championship. The horse, later sold to Chris Kelly, performed well to finish equal first in the Trial Stakes and equal fifth in the actual Foxhunter Championship.

I asked Geoff how he felt when offered the ride on Forge Mill and he told me he was not at all keen on the idea. It was a lot to take on, there would be so much to live up to. He had ridden five or six Grade 'A' horses in his time, all of which he'd made and brought on himself, but certainly nothing approaching the standard of Pennwood Forge Mill.

Valerie Hartill had been getting Forge Mill fit at home and jumping him over a few small fences. On Wednesday, 18th May, Fred Hartill gave Geoff a ring and asked him to come over as he had a horse for him to try. Geoff duly arrived and was surprised to see Forge Mill pulled out of his stable. Geoff said, "What's this?", to which Fred replied,

"I'd like you to have a ride on him". After much persuasion Geoff got on Forgie and after riding him round for a while popped him over a few small fences. "Right, we'll take him to a show on Saturday", said Fred Hartill. Geoff kept saying "No" but Fred Hartill is nothing if not persistent and each time Geoff got up to go he would bring up another subject. Then somebody came into the room and Fred Hartill told them Geoff was going to take Forge Mill to a show on the Saturday and Geoff found he was beaten and duly agreed!

Their appearance in the Open Jumping at Crane Hill Show in Warwickshire on 21st May caused a stir of excitement amongst the spectators at this relatively small show, organised so efficiently by Anthony and Ann Sabin at their Wellesbourne home. Nobody knew Forge Mill was jumping there until just before the class for he was substituted at the last possible moment for another Pennwood horse. All the Hartill connections were anxious about how he would go; it would be terrible if he and Geoff made a hash of things. They needn't have worried for he jumped a lovely clear in the first round. In the jump-off, going a bit too strongly into the combination, Geoff steadied him a little too much with the result they had the first part down for four faults which placed them 8th. Everybody was well pleased with this performance and by now Geoff was beginning to think that perhaps the idea was not such a bad one after all! Course builder at Crane Hill that day was Norman James and he recollects, "I was very surprised when I saw Geoff come into the ring on Pennwood Forge Mill. The partnership got off to a good start and has gone from strength to strength, it was quite a step up for Geoff and I'm pleased he's made the grade because he used to jump horses for me".

Geoff tells me that Forgie is unlike any other horse he's ever ridden, you have to ride him in a totally different manner. You wouldn't think the horse you jump at home, who doesn't impress at all, could be the same horse you jump in the ring when he becomes alive. The trial at Crane Hill had whetted Geoff's appetite so they took Pennwood

Forge Mill to the Staffordshire County Show, covering themselves in glory by winning two big classes, the Jenkinson Stakes and the Bass Worthington Bicentenary Competition. He was very impressive against opposition which included several Olympic and International riders. Geoff recalls, "To win at Staffordshire County meant a lot to me as it was there that I had my first county show win with Buccaneer XXI. To go to my local county show and win the two main classes was quite something. It was marvellous to win the first day, but to come out and win again the next was unbelievable".

' The pair went to three or four other shows, including the Three Counties where, after going so well together from the start, they suddenly didn't click. This was bound to happen at some stage for perhaps they'd started off too well — you can't always win. On the few occasions when he's not in the ribbons Forge Mill gets very upset, he always expects to have to go into the arena to collect his rosette.

Next came the biggest question of their short time together, the Pro/Am Championships at Cardiff. This was Geoff's first international show and he walked the course for the first leg of the Professional Championships with Steve Hadley. He encountered the biggest fences he'd ever been asked to jump and on leaving the ring remarked to Fred Hartill that the fences were very big. Fred replied, "It's all right, the horse has jumped seven foot three inches" to which Geoff quipped back, "I know, but I haven't!".

The sportsmanship to be found in the world of show jumping was underlined here for Geoff found many of his fellow competitors only too pleased to help him. Harvey Smith and David Broome were ready to give advice but it was Ted Edgar who gave him the most help and encouragement. Ted told me, "Geoff was very nervous to be riding such a good horse. He needed a lift so I was pleased to help him and give him a bit of advice". It was, in fact, Ted who pointed out to Fred Hartill that he had a good rider for Forge Mill right on his doorstep for he'd seen Geoff go to a show with six donkeys (in a manner of speaking) and win six first prizes. Ted considers Forge Mill one of the most genuine and consistent horses we've ever had.

Forgie is a bit like an elephant, for he never forgets. The previous year at Cardiff he suffered a bad fall with Paddy and he remembered this — not wanting to go near a fence placed in the same spot. The five clear rounds in the first leg did not include Forge Mill, the winner being Ted Edgar with Everest Amigo. However, Forgie pulled up in the table on the second day when reaching the final to finish seventh of the nine in the jump-off.

Geoff still considers the course built by Alan Ball for the third leg to be the biggest ever. The double was a big parallel over a water ditch to a high vertical. The combination was big and the course finished over the water. On this morning Ted Edgar gave Geoff a good talking to and really put him on the right road. He told him he must have more aggression and ride in a more attacking manner. Geoff felt that until then he had been nursing the horse and he took Ted's advice and has never looked back. Jumping brilliantly he was one of four clear and in the jump-off was again faultless in 43·8 seconds to win the third leg from Caroline Bradley on Tric Trac and Freddie Welch and Rossmore. He finished sixth overall for the professional title which went to Ted Edgar, with his wife Liz completing a great double by taking the amateur crown.

Having missed entries at a lot of shows Forge Mill did not jump again until the Wales and West Show. Here the last qualifier for the Royal International Horse Show took place. Forge Mill not having competed at many shows was not qualified but he made sure of his place at Wembley by winning the Area International Trial at a show dominated by the Everest Stud who won virtually everything else.

Forge Mill likes the Royal Show at Stoneleigh, reacting to the crowd whose darling he is, being a comparatively local horse. Here he finished seventh in the Everest Double Glazing Competition on the first day. On the Wednesday he kept his fine record at Stoneleigh by winning the Hennessy

Cognac Stakes for the second time. Geoff feels that Forgie's great asset is his ability to be able to pick up and go and it was this which won him the class. The last line had caught out many. Stretching out he only put in three strides between the second and third elements of the combination when others were taking four and with his deceptive turn of foot clocked 40·9 seconds, two seconds faster than his nearest rivals, Tony Newbery and Warwick III.

Caroline Bradley and the Countess of Inchcape's scopey chesnut Berna (since sold abroad) won the B.S.J.A. National Championship with the only clear round; Forgie with the fastest four faults finishing second. This clinched the Leading Rider award for Geoff with Caroline taking the Ladies' prize. Ted Edgar must have been cursing himself for giving Geoff such good advice, for his protégé Nick Skelton finished second to Geoff for this title.

Next on the agenda was Buckingham where the ground was like concrete so Geoff only put Forgie over the practice fence twice. He went super in the ring over a big course to score from Ted Edgar. From Buckingham to Billing, where it was again Nick's turn to take second place behind Geoff. Ted's good advice was losing the Everest Stud money! Forgie really played to the crowd at Billing for he loves an audience.

Geoff had never competed at the Royal International Horse Show but they got off to a good start, reaching the jump-off for the Horse and Hound Cup on the opening night but having the wall down for four faults in the final. They came close to recapturing the King George V Gold Cup (won by Paddy on Forge Mill in 1973) when finishing equal third on the Wednesday evening. It went, for the record fourth time, to David Broome, this time riding Harris Carpets' Philco, from Ferdi Tyteca of Belgium on Ransome. I asked Geoff if he had experienced any difficulties in changing to the confined space of the Empire Pool after jumping outside all summer. He feels it doesn't make any difference with Forge Mill as he rises to the occasion and loves the atmosphere but he thinks there could be problems at first with most horses.

The other riders used to pull his leg about having a cushy life with only one horse to jump when they had several. Forgie doesn't need a lot of work during the day and likes more than anything to just potter around meeting people. Forge Mill and Geoff Glazzard had been knocking on the door all week at the Royal International and were perhaps unlucky not to have done better, the curved gate proving their bogey fence.

On the way home they took in the Northampton Show, winning the A.I.T. which qualified them for the following year's Royal International. It was at this show that Forgie suddenly spied his 'Mum' (Mrs. Hartill) through the crowds and, dragging Valerie, ploughed through to see her, hoping for a bite of her ice cream!

Wales was next stop where at the Anglesey Show they had the smallest fence on the course down when some motorcycles started up just as Forgie came to the fence. The following day at Butlins' Pwllheli Show he won his class, thus earning a tilt at the Wembley final. At Ruthin Forgie went very stuffily, proving very unco-operative and not trying. Geoff gave him a slap on the shoulder to wake him up but Forgie did not like this and when they got to the water jump he made no attempt to clear it, just jumping the brush and landing plonk in the water! Geoff decided the best thing to do was to retire him and luckily he could see the funny side of it and came out of the ring grinning all over his face. Forgie was not going to be told what to do.

The Shrewsbury Show was included in the homeward journey, stopping off here to win a big class on the second day, again by taking one less stride in the combination so great is Forge Mill's ability. It was during their Welsh trip that Geoff learnt that he had been selected to go to Rotterdam with Pennwood Forge Mill as members of the British team. Geoff had to rush off to get his passport and there was a wild panic because it only arrived two days before they were due to leave. Fred Hartill had been saying all season that he should get one just in case he was chosen but Geoff had not wanted to tempt providence. Geoff and Fred Hartill flew out, while Forge Mill and Valerie travelled by road and sea in Caroline Bradley's box.

I asked Geoff how it felt to represent your country for the first time and wondered if he was nervous. "I was very proud to be riding for Great Britain but I didn't feel unduly nervous. I can have nerves in the collecting ring but as soon as I walk into the ring I forget all about them and want to get on with the job." In their first competition Geoff and Forge Mill finished second in a speed class to Eric Wauters of Belgium riding Va Petit Mousse who went like a bat out of hell. Fred Hartill remembers that Geoff was very calm and collected which pleased him — Geoff treated it just like a show at home.

Ronnie Masserella, the Chef d'Equipe, had a difficult job choosing the team for the Nations Cup, the problem was knowing who to leave out. In the end he selected Malcolm Pyrah riding the Olympic horse Law Court, Ted Edgar with Everest Amigo, Geoff and Pennwood Forge Mill and Caroline Bradley with her brilliant stallion Marius. Harvey Smith, who was not included in the squad, walked the course with Geoff and was very helpful. Geoff feels that you should listen to all the advice given you but when it boils down to it the decision is yours alone. The pressure is greater in the Nations Cup because you feel you'd be not only letting yourself down but other people. As the choice was so close, Geoff knew he had to go in there and really prove his worth. Everybody knew that Pennwood Forge Mill was capable, the question was would Geoff Glazzard make the grade, had he the right temperament?

Geoff did not let himself or his country down, jumping a four-fault round in the first leg. We were lying equal first with Holland on four faults at the end of the first round with Ireland on 12. But British fortunes were to change a lot in the second round. Forge Mill was in the water and also had the upright planks by the collecting ring down for eight faults, the same score as Everest Amigo. Marius had a bad round of 12 faults and Law Court also had eight. This put us into second place, equal with the home side, behind Ireland. Although we didn't actually win, this second place clinched the 1977 President's Trophy for Great Britain. As so often in Rotterdam, it was wet, and conditions were bad for the Grand Prix, in which Forge Mill jumped two four-fault rounds to finish eighth. He had done well in his first show abroad with Geoff.

Back home they won the much sought after B.S.J.A. International (formerly Olympic) Trial at British Timken against strong opposition. Alan Ball had built a truly International course which found out many of the 29 starters, four of the first seven retiring. Six went clear to the final with Geoff riding Forge Mill really well to go clear in 43·5 seconds.

They went on to win the Area International Trial at Leicester City. Radio Rentals were running a Points Championship during 1977 with the conclusion being reached at Wembley and after this success Geoff realised they were in with a chance. A good win in the Radio Rentals class at the City of Birmingham Show added yet more points and it was here that Geoff won three classes on three different horses, the others being My Stranger (Grades 'B' and 'C') and Pennwood Sandstorm (City of Birmingham Championship). Despite the fact that they'd gone well at Birmingham on the first two days they decided to foresake the local show on the Sunday and travel instead to Harrogate for Lister Welch's show. It was disastrous as everything went wrong and to make matters worse it poured with rain.

They were second at Burghley in the Raleigh Championship to Tim Grubb riding Chicago. Geoff had been hoping for more points but came down to the Radio Rentals fence too complacently with the result that Forge Mill (a wily old devil in his old age!) stopped, shooting Geoff up his neck.

Somehow he managed to get back into the saddle and continued his round. "That will teach me to be too cocky", said Geoff as he came out of the ring. They did no good at the Camberley Show but finished second in Newbury's Area International Trial to Ann Smith and Rushgreen.

Indoors once more the scene switched to the Everest Double Glazing Championships held for the first time that year at Park Farm, Northwood. Forgie didn't get very inspired here for there was not a big crowd to carry him. However, he did enjoy his rides round the cross-country course with Valerie, so much did they liven him up that Geoff couldn't hold him in the ring and was nearly bucked off! Geoff came away from Park Farm not thinking much of his chances at Wembley the following week.

His doubts were, however, very short-lived for in the Butlins Championship on the opening night of the 1977 Horse of the Year Show, Geoff Glazzard and Pennwood Forge Mill tied with no less than David Broome riding Heatwave. Both clocked identical times of 28·9 seconds in an exciting jump-off which had the Wembley crowds sitting on the edge of their seats. David had also qualified Philco for the final and, third to go, they sped round in 29·4 seconds to take the lead in what most people thought was an unbeatable time. Forge Mill then outjumped him to clock 28·9 seconds, a time which even the maestro David Broome could not better, although he did equal it with Heatwave. Winning this class gave Geoff great pleasure, it meant a lot to him to tie with David Broome, who had so much experience whilst Geoff had so little. Forge Mill had risen to the occasion yet again, as soon as he entered the arena for the jump-off the crowd had cheered and Forgie pricked his ears and set off for one of his classic rounds, really cutting, corners. The show could not have got off to a better start for Geoff and Forgie.

It was at Wembley that the fate of the Radio Rentals Points Championships was to be decided and following a third in this valuable event (behind Eddie Macken and

Caroline Bradley) they wound up equal second with David Broome in the points table, behind Marion Mould. The pair jumped consistently all week, finishing eighth in the Leading Show Jumper of the Year, a title it would have been marvellous to see Pennwood Forge Mill win, and wound up equal fourth in the International Spurs Points Award. Geoff came near to winning the Foxhunter Championship at the 1977 show with Fred Hartill's Pennwood Drumadora. They did a very fast round in the jump-off but a fence down put them second behind Mallowry Spens and Port O'Paddy.

Forgie was rested until a week before Olympia when he went to Mill Lodge for a warm-up. Here he lacked the sparkle needed to head for London with any great confidence, although he did manage to win a small class. Raymond Brooks-Ward and his team stage Olympia as a happy-go-lucky Christmas show with the pantomime, glitter and Christmas carols lending a festive air to the occasion. Geoff and Pennwood Forge Mill finished their first season together by being placed equal third in the Norwich Union Turkey Stakes and equal third in the Grand Prix, won by David Broome and Philco.

It was at Olympia that the President's Trophy was presented to team manager Ronnie Masserella by H.R.H. Princess Alexandra. We had scored 35½ points to Germany's 32 and Ireland's 31, and all the horses which had contributed to our success came into the arena for the ceremony. Forgie loves parades and proudly wore his sash around his neck and pranced around the arena like a two-year-old.

Although Pennwood Forge Mill did not start his campaign until May and was only lightly jumped all season he still finished third in the list of National Prizewinners. He was 16th in the International List and eighth in the Combined. Geoff Glazzard and Pennwood Forge Mill had certainly proved their worth during the 1977 season and the rider had no regrets about being persuaded to ride the horse!

13

ANOTHER HORSE AND HOUND CUP

Forgie enjoyed a nice long rest after the 1977 Olympia Show, being turned out by day with the faithful Magpie and coming into his stable each night. His first show of the 1978 season was at Chippenham and Charlton, held in Lord and Lady Suffolk's lovely park near Malmesbury in Wiltshire, on May 5th-7th. Geoff was well pleased with Forgie's performance on the first day for the courses at this new show were bigger than he had anticipated for so early in the season.

He jumped well in the first class for just four faults, having travelled to the show in his smart new Pennwood lorry. Another girl was helping Valerie with the horses and Valerie asked her to give Forgie a bite of grass after he'd jumped and then put him back on the lorry. When she returned she was surprised to see him still standing at the bottom of the ramp refusing to go up and looking rather stubborn. He sums people up very quickly and knows when he can get away with something!

Gill Kelly is coached by Geoff and, riding the former Pennwood horse, Pepperpot, she distinguished herself in the following day's Area International Trial by defeating a strong field, Forge Mill finishing ninth. The next day, however, belonged to Pennwood Forge Mill when he walked away with the Partnerplan Grand Prix from Derek Ricketts riding Mrs. Lock's Nice 'n' Easy.

Preparation was unhurried and his next show was Shrewsbury and West Midland on May 17th-18th when he finished second in the A.I.T., beaten by two-tenths of a second, to Malcolm Pyrah and Law Court. A trip followed to Northumberland to the North of England Equestrian Centre at Stannington, run by show jumper Malcolm Bowey. Forge Mill once more maintained his consistency in A.I.T.s by finishing fourth and was equal sixth in the Mercedes-Benz sponsored Grand Prix. He was going really well in the jump-off but just had the brick out of the curved wall. Valerie remembers that it was dull and cold for this show and on arriving after the long drive from Wolverhampton they couldn't find their stables.

Perhaps Geoff had been hoping for great things at Staffordshire County but things seldom work out as planned and he didn't go well here, the best they could manage being an equal ninth. At the Bath and West Show Forgie was too full of himself on the first morning so Geoff put him in the little speed class later that day. Now that he is older he holds decided views on jumping in more than one class per day and just didn't try one little bit, knocking up a cricket score of 19 faults! He was determined to knock them down, you could see the mulish expression on his face, and Geoff came out looking very red in the face! He had settled by the third day when he proved a highly popular winner of the Radio Rentals Stakes, jumping the only clear in a four-cornered jump-off.

At Butlins Qualifying Show he ran out at one fence and it was soon after this that it was discovered he had a hook tooth which had cut his mouth. They got his teeth filed and this put him back on a winning streak and he won the Area International Trial at Vauxhall Motors Show at Luton.

Geoff also went well here on his other horses, carrying off the Leading Rider Award. Leicester City followed the next day when Forgie was placed fourth in the Everest Double Glazing class.

Staged in a tranquil setting nestling beneath the Malvern Hills, the Three Counties Show took place the following week when Forge Mill was seventh in the A.I.T. on the final day. As the ground was so hard he was only jumped in this one class throughout the show.

Next it was time once more for the Pro/Am Championships at Cardiff Castle. As Geoff had found the previous year the courses were again big but he and Forge Mill fully held their own as they had in 1977. In the opening leg of the Professional title they finished third in an eight-cornered jump-off with four faults in 43·2 seconds to Caroline Bradley on Tigre and Lionel Dunning on his new 'find' Jungle Bunny. Forgie finished ninth in the second leg which went to his former partner Paddy MacMahon riding Gollanite (later to become Gollanite Hoeschst). Really trying his heart out, Pennwood Forge Mill captured the third leg for the second year running. He really jumped, putting everything he had into it, and the spectators carried him to victory, for he is a great favourite with the Welsh crowd. There was a record attendance for this third leg held in glorious sunny weather. His ninth place had robbed him of the title for he finished equal second with Caroline Bradley, behind David Broome, the 1978 Professional Champion.

A break followed until he went to the Wales and West Show at the beginning of July as a pipe-opener for the Royal Show. On the first day of the Royal, in very greasy conditions, he slipped at the second fence and gave himself a fright. His confidence having taken a bit of a knock he came away from Stoneleigh without a major first prize for the first time in six years (although he did win the Radio Rentals Qualifier in Ring 'A'). Nevertheless he was still in the prize money, including eighth in the Hennessy, third in the Everest Double Glazing and fourth in the final of the Radio

Rentals Championship (incorporating the National Championship) which went to Yorkshire in the form of Graham Fletcher and Buttevant Boy.

'Four-faultitis' was again their problem at the Great Yorkshire Show at Harrogate but fortunately on the opening night of the Royal International Show at Wembley it deserted them and Forgie strode away with the Horse and Hound Cup and £800. It was a highly exciting contest with ten horses clear (although Debbie Johnsey then withdrew Croupier). Forge Mill, fourth to go, sauntered into the ring looking as though a bomb wouldn't move him. But when Geoff picked up the reins and urged him into a canter it was a different matter, he pricked his ears and shot through the start. Twisting and turning like a stag he jumped clear in an incredible 33·7 seconds. Geoff had to live through the suspense of four other horses but he was home and dry for none could equal Forgie's great time. The handsome trophy, which he had won in 1973 with Paddy, thus returned to Pennwood to be displayed with all his other trophies in the special Forge Mill window at the shop. "He's great, you just always know he'll try", said his jubilant rider after this Wembley win.

A win at the Royal International or Horse of the Year Show means a lot to every rider. There are many of our leading ones who have been going for years and have never won a class there. Out of two shows with Pennwood Forge Mill Geoff had won a class at each, not a bad record. It is interesting to note that on each occasion it was on the opening night, thus underlining the theory that his jumping goes off when he can't get his daily grass and relaxation of being turned out now that he is older.

In the King George V Gold Cup on the Wednesday evening they again reached the final to finish equal fourth, the victor being Jeff McVean of Australia with his good mare Claret when Graham Fletcher was forced to withdraw Cool Customer from the final due to lameness. The valuable John Player Grand Prix went for an unbelievable seventh time to Harvey Smith, Forgie finishing seventh in this two-round competition. The special groom's prize was awarded to Hob (who does the Everest horses for the Edgars) with Valerie in second place. The judge commented that Forgie's tail was too long but Valerie would never make it shorter for it is one of his trade marks.

Chris Coldrey presides over the Arena North with great efficiency and Geoff and Forge Mill paid a visit to their International Show at the end of July. The Americans were competing here as preparation for the World Championships in Aachen and they really held their own. Geoff told me that Forgie went really topping throughout the show. He was equal third in the Area International Trial and second in the speed class to American visitor Buddy Brown with Viscount. He had held the lead until nearly the end when the American pair flew round. This forward-thinking show stages a Show Jumping Bass Grand National over a 17-fence course. Forgie reached the second jump-off along with 16 others and was unlucky not to win, recording the fastest time but having the fence down on top of the bank to drop to seventh place. The winner was John Whitaker with Ryan's Son.

Geoff has never visited Hickstead but intended to go to the 1978 British Derby Meeting in August. However, when he heard that they'd again been selected to represent Britain in Rotterdam the plan was scrapped. Off on the Welsh circuit as usual at this time of year, he finished second in the Area International Trial at Ruthin on 5th August despite Forgie falling in the practice area and frightening himself. Six days later he went to Shrewsbury, having a new travelling companion in Arksey. This big scopey bay is to my mind a horse of tremendous ability. A former in-hand hunter winner in Dublin he was previously jumped by Tim Grubb, Malcolm Pyrah and, during the early part of 1978, by David Broome. At Shrewsbury he finished equal sixth in the Everest Double Glazing along with Forgie and two others.

117

Geoff found he had problems adapting to the very different style of Arksey. He is a complete contrast to Forge Mill, going on a short bouncy stride whereas Forge Mill likes to flow on lengthening his stride. Geoff feels it was perhaps Forge Mill who suffered the most because he started trying to make him jump off a short stride at times and it just didn't work. Arksey has now been sold and is going well for former leading junior Michael Mac, in his first season in Adult Classes.

At Anglesey Show Pennwood Forge Mill won his sixteenth Area International Trial — quite a record, there can be few, if any, horses to have equalled it, let alone bettered it. Arksey finished in fifth place. During August an enterprising new show was staged on Wolverhampton Racecourse called the Midshires Horse Show with a £1,000 first prize being put up by the Midshires Building Society for the main event, the Masters' Championship. The organizers put on a parade for this class and the horse which got the loudest cheer was Pennwood Forge Mill who is stabled only a few miles away. Much to their dismay the local hero had a fence down in the first round but Arksey jumped a lovely clear over Alan Oliver's big track to reach the five horse jump-off. He went really well to go clear again but in a slower time than Graham Fletcher and Cool Customer and Sally Mapleson (the young Essex rider) on the Dutch-bred Con-Brio, to take third place.

Over the sea to Rotterdam where for once the clerk of the weather was kind to them, apart from the last day, which made the show all the more enjoyable. They travelled with the Dunnings (Lionel was riding Jungle Bunny and Wiffenpoof) and the other members of the team were three young riders earning their first British caps: David Bowen with Scorton and Brindle Boy, the Scottish rider John Brown with Tangier Angus and Fymac, and Anna Fawdry with Little Rascal and Barley Wine. During the evenings, Geoff, David and John got up to some high jinks and one of their most enjoyable receptions was the one held on a boat going round the harbour, with good food and plenty of wine. Out exercising in the woods Valerie gave Forgie his head and he went straight to the collecting ring area so keen was he to get on with the game. Chef d'Equipe was Colonel Guy Wathen and he told me "I first met Forge Mill on the team with Paddy at Geneva in 1973 when I was Chef d'Equipe and again in Lucerne during the 1974 season. I've naturally followed his career with interest. He's a most marvellous sort of solid, reliable horse who nevertheless could pull off the occasional feat of brilliance. He was in our Rotterdam team in 1977 as well as 1978, with Geoff Glazzard, and is jumping just as well as ever."

In a strong eight-team contest for the Nations Cup our riders finished second to the Americans, gaining valuable points to put us back in the hunt for the President's Trophy. Everybody was worried that the course would be enormous but it proved, although large, not unduly big although it did pose a few problems. Our team consisted of John Brown with Tangier Angus, clear and four faults (at the water); David Bowen on Brindle Boy 12 and 12; Lionel Dunning and Jungle Bunny 4 and 3; Pennwood Forge Mill (first to go) had four faults in the first and then jumped a clear despite the pouring rain. Apart from Forge Mill our team was very inexperienced and we had done well to take second place ahead of the Canadians and Belgians.

For the first Grand Prix Qualifying competition Geoff was issued with instructions to go steadily over the big course and this he did to finish sixth. The second day's qualifying course was even bigger and there were many complaints but the course remained unaltered. Only three clear rounds were recorded, from van Paesschen of Belgium on Porche, Mike Matz of the USA with Sandor and Canada's Ian Millar riding Brother Sam. Friday's qualifier was contested over a 5 ft. 3 in. course and Forge Mill going early set an unbeatable target to win. David Bowen and Brindle Boy with the last fence down finished fifth.

Four British riders had qualified for the Grand Prix with

Jungle Bunny being one of seven clears through to the second round. They were joined by the seven on four faults who included Forge Mill and Scorton. Jungle Bunny had two down this time but Scorton went round fast and clear for eighth place in his first Grand Prix. Dear old Forge Mill, gallant as ever, galloped round clear and fast and was placed fourth. The final jump-off between the three double clears provided a fitting climax to the show with victory going to the stylish Canadian Terry Leibel riding Sympatico from Nelson Pessoa on Moet et Chandon Chopin and Ian Millar on Brother Sam. It was in Rotterdam that they met some well-known racing drivers who were thrilled to meet such a famous horse and asked if they could pat him.

Arksey had also travelled to Rotterdam and they came back in Lionel's lorry, staying overnight with him before being collected at the Leicester City Show. Forgie didn't jump here as he was tired after the journey. The nearby City of Birmingham Show followed and then on to the Wales and West Show for the Welsh Jumping Derby. Jon Doney's course had fences ranging from 4 ft. 6 in. to 5 ft. 6 in. and included a double of ditches, a Devil's Dyke, the big bank (standing at 10 ft. 6 in. but less steep than Hickstead) followed one stride after landing by vertical rustics and finishing over a wall. The fence on top of the bank stands at 4 ft. 6 in. which is much bigger than the one on top of the Hickstead bank. From a high-class field of 43 Forgie finished equal fourth with three others on four faults. David Broome, at last beating the voodoo on his home ground, ran out the winner on Sportsman with Derek Ricketts second on Nice 'n' Easy and Graham Fletcher third with Buttevant Boy. Forgie jumped really well and his rider admits it was his fault they had four faults. He had never descended such a bank and he brought Forgie down right to the bottom instead of jumping off from a little way up. Consequently he got right under the fence just one stride away and had it down. The sun was shining, the band of the Royal Regiment of Wales rang out across the arena and this Welsh Derby was the highlight of the meeting organised by the Broomes. At Camberley Show Forgie did no good but, as in 1977, he finished second in Newbury's Area International Trial. It was for this show that he was stabled at Bobby Black's Simms Stud and he had to go and have a look round to make sure he approved before Valerie could do anything with him. He's a very inquisitive fellow is Pennwood Forge Mill.

He is able to get his daily bite of grass and have a wander round at Park Farm and, appreciating this, he won the Solaramic Championship on the second night of the Everest Double Glazing Championships. The course had some awkward turns and Forgie, second last to go in a nine-horse barrage, went clear to win by 1·7 seconds from David Broome and Sportsman. There was life in the old boy yet!

He was a bit off form at the Horse of the Year Show and the best he achieved was a sixth place in the Butlins and an eighth in the Sunday Times Cup. A new addition to the show jumping calendar in 1978 was the Stoneleigh Autumn Championships held at the National Equestrian Centre in October. Forgie and Arksey were stabled at Stoneleigh for the show to save travelling, with Valerie in charge. On the first two days Forgie experienced some trouble coping with the combinations but on the third day he finished fourth in the Lancia Qualifier although once more it was the treble which found him out. Arksey went really well in the Puissance to tie with Rowland Fernyhough on Bouncer, both clearing 6 ft. 10 in. over the big Wembley wall in use outside London for the first time.

Forgie was then turned out for a short rest before a tilt at the Harris Carpets Daily Express Masters contest at Harwood Hall in Essex. In the first round Forgie and Geoff jumped a lovely clear but things did not go right in the second round and they had two fences down for eight faults. Possibly Geoff was still experiencing some difficulty in adapting to the completely differing styles of Forge Mill and Arksey. Harvey Smith ran out the winner on Sanyo San Mar, beating Caroline Bradley and Tigre by 3·5 seconds.

When the B.S.J.A. published their list of Top Twenty Horses Pennwood Forge Mill's name featured once more. He was tenth in the list of National winners, twelfth in the International and eleventh overall. He has certainly won a lot of money for the Hartills and his riders.

Following Harwood Hall Forgie had nearly a month off before the Christmas Olympia Show. This is a 'fun' sort of event with everybody (riders, course builders, etc.) entering into the spirit of things and taking part in the fancy dress jumping and camel and donkey racing. Mary Chipperfield's ever-popular camels appeared at each performance under Chief of the Camel Corps (alias Ted Edgar) with the victims including Lucinda Prior-Palmer, B.S.J.A. senior course builder Alan Ball and various show jumpers. Highlight of the show was the fast-moving Activity Ride put on by the Metropolitan Police Mounted Branch, with horses jumping through fire and their riders shedding their jackets and taking off the saddles to the appropriate strains of 'The Stripper'!

Raymond Brooks-Ward and his team work very hard to put on five days of great entertainment. Raymond is Joint-Master of the Enfield Chace Hounds and his pony club stage a pantomime each year, the 1978 one being 'Cinderella'. Each performance closed with the grande finale, 'A Victorian Christmas in the City of London', produced by Dorian Williams, with snow falling gently on the assembled company as Father Christmas arrived with his sleigh full of presents.

Thirty-nine of the world's top show jumpers took part, including all Britain's stars and 11 invited riders from abroad, jumping for a total of nearly £22,000 in prize money.

For the show jumping fraternity much of the year is spent away from home, rather like a travelling circus. Very often they do not return to base for weeks on end at the height of the season. But they certainly do not slum it, living in caravans and boxes with very luxurious living quarters with running hot water, gas fires and TV. At Olympia the caravans and boxes are parked together under cover in one of the main halls just a few minutes' walk from the stables which are also under cover. The hustle and bustle goes on until late at night (or early in the morning!) with many a party taking place. But the next morning the grooms have to be up early to feed their charges. Then back for a quick bite of breakfast before mucking out and grooming. If the horse is not being jumped until the evening he will need to be exercised, then there is the tack to clean, the bandages and overreach boots to be washed. So there's little chance for relaxation or even sometimes to get a proper meal. Often the horse will not finish jumping until 11 p.m. so it's after midnight by the time the weary groom gets to bed. A long hard day and certainly not as glamorous as some people may think.

On the opening night of the 1978 Olympia Show Forge Mill took part in the Norwich Union Turkey Stakes but it was obvious as soon as he came into the arena that he wasn't in his most co-operative mood and he had two fences down. The next day he was in a better mood to record one of only six clears in the Harris Carpet Stakes. Perhaps age was beginning to tell for although he had gone so well first time he found the effort too much in the jump-off and, standing back off the double, had it down to finish fifth. The winner was Robert Smith, aged 17, riding Sanyo Video (formerly called Upton and then Pennwood Holvair when ridden by Paddy MacMahon).

Saturday's Radio Rentals Christmas Stakes saw Geoff Glazzard dumped by Forgie for the first time. He was going well over this big track until they came to the treble across the middle of the arena. He went in a bit stuffily and caught his back leg between the poles of the second part. Caught off balance Forgie stopped at the third element, decanting Geoff into the poles with a crash. Back on board once more Geoff drove the horse through at the second attempt in an attacking manner and then sensibly retired. The winner of

123

this was Nick Skelton on Maybe.

Saturday evening was the Radio Rentals Puissance with Arksey and Geoff Glazzard being one of ten clears. But in the next round with the wall standing at 6 ft. 6 in. they failed to clear it. The winner once more was Nick Skelton, this time with the German-bred Everest Lastic.

Then came the exciting news that there would be a unique happening, an attempt at the British High Jump Record. This record of 7 ft. 6½ in. was set up by Don Beard (brother of Curly) at Olympia 41 years previously riding Swank. The High Jump takes place not over the big wall (that is a Puissance) but over sloping poles on top of wattles. Seven took up the challenge although they did not, surprisingly, include Harvey Smith. They started over 6 ft. 4 in. and, allowed three attempts, all went clear, although Double Brandy and Graham Fletcher had it down first time and he was subsequently withdrawn from the next round. At 6 ft. 9½ in. all bar Freddie Welch and Rossmore made it, although Bouncer had to have two attempts.

It was then up to 7 ft. $7\frac{5}{16}$ in. (over 10 in. higher than the previous round) for five brave men to attempt to break the record. Geoff Glazzard was in the unenviable position of having to go first. Arksey had three good tries but took the top pole off each time. Then it was the turn of Lastic. Nick took the big grey horse in too fast at this first try and he crashed right through, scattering poles in all directions. At his second attempt he came a bit closer but Nick was not keen to have another crack. However, Ted Edgar had other ideas and told Nick to have another go. This he did and the pair cleared the enormous fence to set up a new British record. The crowd went wild and everybody at Olympia that night was proud to have been present when Nick Skelton, just a few weeks off his twenty-first birthday, had achieved such a fantastic feat. None of the three who followed, Tony Holden with Mr. Volvo, Rowland Fernyhough and Bouncer, or Derek Ricketts and Denham Hills, could match this performance. It was a marvellous evening for the young

Warwickshire lad and his mentors, Liz and Ted Edgar of the Everest Stud.

Following the way he had gone on Saturday, Geoff decided to put Forgie in the smaller class on Sunday. The course for this was, however, very big and some of the riders withdrew in protest. Forgie was one of 12 clears but in the jump-off he had two fences down.

The top 24 riders throughout the show qualify for the Grand Prix and Forge Mill was amongst the starters. Perhaps feeling the strain of jumping these big fences in a confined space all week Forgie was soon in trouble and Geoff wisely retired him.

But he still had to make one more appearance in the Olympia arena. Following our win in the Antwerp Nations Cup in early September we had retained the President's Trophy and as one of the 19 horses which had contributed to our win Pennwood Forge Mill and Geoff Glazzard came into the ring for the presentation. Each horse was accompanied by its owner, a nice gesture for where would show jumping be today without all the owners who very often get little recognition? To them and all the generous sponsors we owe a great debt.

Pennwood Forge Mill stood stock still, looking as usual serene and calm, as the trophy was presented to Team Manager Ronnie Masserella. He was perhaps dreaming of the rest he would now enjoy turned out with his friend Magpie.

14

THE FORGIE FAN CLUB

Pennwood Forge Mill has millions of fans both young and old alike and hardly a week passes without somebody coming to Pennwood especially to see him. At shows his stable is always one of the most popular for show jumping enthusiasts.

Forgie has received many fan letters during his career and at the time of the 1972 Olympics and the European Championships the following year, Paddy would get them in dozens, especially from people bemoaning the fact that Forgie and Paddy had been left out of our Olympic team. At Christmas, Forgie gets lots of cards and presents and the postman is kept busy delivering gifts such as sugar lumps in matchboxes, carrots, chocolates and, of course, 'Polos' galore — his consumption must be one of the highest! One of his regular visitors is a local lady, Mrs. Rogers, who comes to see him before the bigger shows and on his return. She is a very welcome visitor and always brings him a box of his favourite chocolates.

As you know, Forgie likes attention so thrives on all the visitors. Probably his greatest fan is Sedgley resident Jack

Phillips. Wearing well for his 79 years and very alert, Jack never goes anywhere without his three photographs of Forgie. He transfers them from jacket to jacket ("Not that I've got that many", quips he) and also keeps lots of cuttings at home. The three pictures are: Her Majesty The Queen presenting the King George V Gold Cup to Paddy; Forgie putting in a great leap over the Hickstead water (see photograph number 21 in this book); and Geoff jumping him at Wembley. Jack was a great friend of Fred Hartill's father, often accompanying him to dog shows, where he did very well with his cocker spaniels. Like Fred and Janet Hartill he is sad that Fred's father did not live to see Forge Mill become famous. In his local pub, The Swan at Sedgley, Jack always defends Forgie if he has a fence down, and gets teased unmercifully by the other inhabitants for they know how fond he is of the horse. If Forgie doesn't make it through to the jump-off he won't bother to watch the rest, preferring to switch off and retire to bed.

One or two of the local pubs don't have television and on the nights when show jumping is being screened they are nearly empty for everybody likes to follow the fortunes of their local horse. Just a few doors away from Pennwood Saddlery is The Old Stag's Head pub and here they have recently opened a Pennwood Forge Mill lounge, with photographs of Forgie adorning the walls.

Last winter a man arrived by bus and asked if he could see Forge Mill because, he said, "Wolves aren't doing very well, so we've got to have something to follow!". Another two of his fans are Mrs. Bodenham, a stalwart of the local church, and 81-year-old Mrs. Priest, both of whom live in Sedgley. Meeting up with their friends and neighbours whilst shopping, everything has to wait while they discuss how Forge Mill went the previous night. If he had four faults there's a full-scale inquest on it! If any of the Hartill family have to visit the doctor the first thing he asks is how is Forge Mill, before enquiring what's wrong with the patient!

Mrs. Bodenham and Mrs. Priest like to go and see Forgie

at home from time to time and, although they're normally early-bedders, if there's show jumping on TV and Forge Mill is performing they'll stay up until all hours. But if he's out of the reckoning, like Jack Phillips they lose interest and switch off. Mrs. Priest told me, "I always think he does his best; if he has four faults it's not his fault, sometimes his tail knocks it down".

There is great rivalry as to whether he should be described as a Sedgley or Wolverhampton horse, but wherever they live the residents of Sedgley, Wolverhampton and surrounding areas certainly have something to be proud of and Forge Mill has nearly as many followers as the famous Wolves.

When I asked people at Olympia and other shows who their favourite horses were the name of Pennwood Forge Mill kept cropping up over and over again. This genuine, down-to-earth character has captured the imagination of the British public over the years and is still as popular as ever. Not only with the public but with the other show-jumping grooms and riders, both at home and abroad, they all love him.

Nor is his fan club confined to this country. For instance, a Canadian couple who saw the 1973 European Championships on TV were very much taken with him. When the husband asked his wife what she would like for an anniversary present she replied, "A trip to England to meet Pennwood Forge Mill". They duly arrived unannounced on the Saturday of the 1974 Grand National asking in the shop, "Is this where Pennwood Forge Mill lives?". Fortunately, Forgie was in residence so the Hartills sat them down and gave them lunch before taking them to meet their hero. Later they all watched the Grand National on television.

An American couple called J. Ray and Emma Patterson came to watch the jumping at Wembley one year and, admiring Forge Mill and Paddy MacMahon, became friendly with the Hartills. Ray kept telling Fred Hartill he must come out to see them in America. At 4 a.m. one day the phone rang, it was Ray inviting Fred out to America for ten days at his expense. He had a great time with Ray telling all his friends that Fred Hartill was an earl — so they quickly dreamt up the name, Frederick, Earl of Sedgley!

On returning home from Penn, a Japanese man, to whom they supply saddlery, sent Forge Mill a lovely musical photograph book for the Hartills to display his pictures. They still have this much treasured possession.

A special Pennwood Forge Mill suite has recently been built at Pennwood, just across the yard from the shop. Here Forgie has his own stable, wash box and souvenir room filled with many of his photographs, press cuttings and rosettes. This is next to his stable with a special partition so that Forgie can put his head through and talk to his visitors.

As I write these words the plan is to retire him during the 1979 Royal International Horse Show after a final tilt at the King George V Gold Cup. He will have a very easy season until then, just jumping at a few selected shows. Although he is only 15 Pennwood Forge Mill has done a great deal of jumping over the past 11 years. It will be very sad to see him go but surely it is better to retire him whilst he's still at the top? With careful preparation he could still win thousands more but old age and wear are beginning to show and he deserves a happy retirement at Pennwood with Magpie. There is nothing worse than seeing a horse which has been at the top deteriorate and Forgie has been a firm favourite with the British public over the past nine years.

Who knows, one day we may see Pennwood Forge Mill back at Wembley in the Personality Parade, his proud head looking round the packed arena where he has delighted the crowds on so many occasions, as for the final Cavalcade Dorian Williams recites Ronald Duncan's traditional tribute "To the Horse" —

"Where in this wide world can man find nobility without pride,
  Friendship without envy, or beauty without vanity?

Here, where grace is laced with muscle
And strength by gentleness confined.

He served without servility,
He has fought without enmity.
There is nothing so powerful,
Nothing less violent;
There is nothing so quick,
Nothing more patient.

England's past has been borne on his back.
All our history is his industry.
We are his heirs, he our inheritance.
Ladies and Gentlemen — THE HORSE!"

These words sum up Pennwood Forge Mill — he has been a great horse who has always given of his best, a trier to the last. He will not be easily forgotten or replaced in the hearts of show jumping fans. May he enjoy a thoroughly deserved and happy retirement.

PENNWOOD FORGE MILL'S MAIN RESULTS

1968 Season (ridden by John Wrathall)
June – 2nd Foxhunter, Staffordshire Show *(his first rosette)*
July – 2nd Foxhunter, Kings Bromley Show
Sept – 3rd Open, Kenilworth

1969 Season (ridden by John Wrathall)
April – Equal 5th Grade C, Hickstead
  – 4th Grade C, Hickstead
  – Equal 7th Grade C, Hickstead
May – Won Grade C, Wollaston Show *(his first win)*
June – Won Grades B & C, Uttoxeter Show
  – Won Open, East Leake Show
July – Won Grades B & C, Northamptonshire County
  – Won Grade B Championship, East of England Show
August – 8th Popular Open, British Timken Show
September – 2nd Adult Championship, City of Birmingham Show

1970 Season (ridden by John Wrathall)
March – 3rd Popular Open, Hickstead
  – Equal 3rd Popular Open, Hickstead
May – 3rd Open, Burley-on-the-Hill Show
  – 2nd Championship, Staffordshire County
June – Equal 5th Area International Trial, Leicester
  – Equal 6th Area International Trial, Cheshire
July – Won Grade A, Liverpool Show
  – 2nd Championship, Royal Lancs Show
October – 6th Dick Turpin Stakes, Horse of the Year Show
  – Equal 7th Wembley Stakes, Section II

1971 Season (ridden by Paddy McMahon)
May – Won Gents Championship, Lincoln Show
  – 4th Radicon Stakes, Royal Windsor Show
  – 4th St. George Stakes, Royal Windsor Show
  – Equal 5th Supreme Championship, Royal Windsor Show
  – 3rd Area International Trial, Shoprshire & West Midland Show
  – Won Area International Trial, Staffordshire County
June – Won Grades A & B, Cheshire County
July – 5th Country Life Cup, Royal International Horse Show
  – 5th Talbot-Ponsonby Trophy, Royal International Horse Show
  – Won Gents Championship, Hull Show
  – Won Area International Trial, Hull Show

133

August – Won Area International Trial, Bakewell Show
     – 2nd Area International Trial, Anglesey Show
     – Won Grand Prix, Ostend *(first show abroad)*
September – 2nd Puissance, Harwood Hall
     – Won Open, Harwood Hall
October – 5th Philips Championship, Horse of the Year Show
     – Won Butlins Gamblers, Horse of the Year Show *(first win at Wembley)*
     – Won Mayor's Plate, Leeuwarden (Holland)
November – 5th class, Geneva
     – 3rd Grand Prix, Vienna
     – 3rd Puissance, Vienna

1972 Season (ridden by Paddy McMahon)

May – 4th Supreme Championship, Rome
     – Won Area International Trial, Aldershot Show
     – 2nd Championship, Staffordshire County
June – Won Gents Championship, Three Counties
July – Won Texaco Championship, Royal Show
     – 2nd Embassy Regal Stakes, Hickstead
     – Equal 2nd Moss Bros. Championship (Puissance), Royal International Horse Show
     – 3rd King George V Gold Cup, Royal International Horse Show
     – 5th Grand Prix, Royal International Horse Show
     – 3rd Daily Mail Cup, Royal International Horse Show
     – Won Saddle of Honour for gaining most points Royal International Show
August – Won Castella Stakes, Hickstead
     – 2nd British Jumping Derby, Hickstead
     – Won Championship, British Timken
     – Won Olympic Trial, British Timken
September – 2nd Himalyan Championship, Everest Double Glazing Championships
     – 2nd Championship, Everest Double Glazing Championships
October – 2nd Norwich Union Stakes, Horse of the Year Show
     – 2nd Sunday Times Cup, Horse of the Year Show
     – Won Ronson Trophy, Horse of the Year Show

1973 Season (ridden by Paddy McMahon)

May – Won Area International Trial, Newark and Notts Show
     – 2nd Area International Trial, Royal Windsor Show
     – Won three classes and second in two others Madrid Show
June – Won Area International Trial, Northern Horse Show
     – Won John Player Grand Prix, Nottinghamshire Show

July — Won Texaco Trophy, Royal Show
 — Won Area International Trial, Royal Show
 — 2nd BMW Championship, Royal Show
 — Won first leg European Championship, Hickstead
 — Equal 2nd second leg European Championship, Hickstead
 — 2nd third leg European Championship, Hickstead
 — Won European Show Jumping Championship Title, Hickstead
 — Won Horse and Hound Cup, Royal International Horse Show
 — Won King George V Gold Cup, Royal International Horse Show
August — Won Puissance, Belfast Show
 — 2nd Grand Prix, Belfast Show
 — 4th Grand Prix of Ireland, Dublin Show
 — Equal 2nd British Jumping Derby, Hickstead
 — Two 3rd places, Rotterdam
September — Won Champion of Champions Competition, St. Gallen,
 plus another class
 — Won Grade A, Lister Welch's Show
October — Won Solaramic Championship, Everest Double Glazing
 Championships
 — 4th Sunday Times Cup, Horse of the Year Show
November — Won one class, 2nd in two others and 3rd Grand Prix,
 Geneva
December — 2nd Turkey Stakes, Dunhill Olympia Show
 — 2nd Victor Ludorum, Dunhill Christmas Show

1974 Season (ridden by Paddy McMahon)
May — Won Merck, Sharp & Dohme Supreme Championship, Royal
 Windsor Show
 — Won Bass Open, Staffordshire County
 — Won Blue Circle Stakes, Bath and West Show
 — Won Equizole Stakes, Bath and West Show
 — Won Wilkinson Sword Class, Aldershot Show
June — Won class, Lucerne
July — 5th Texaco Championship, Royal Show
 — 2nd Dunhill Championship, Royal Show
 — Equal 1st Puissance, Midlands International
August — 3rd Grand Prix of Ireland, Dublin Show
 — 2nd Castella Stakes, Hickstead
 — 2nd Olympic Trial, British Timken Show

1975 Season (ridden by Paddy McMahon)
May — 2nd Radio Rentals Stakes, Devon County

June — Won Area International Trial, South of England Show
  — 4th Professional Championship, Cardiff
  — Won Radio Rentals Stakes, South of England Show
  — 3rd Puissance, Fontainbleau
July — Won Hennessy Championship, Royal Show
  — 3rd Texaco Championship, Royal Show
  — Won Championship, Great Yorkshire
  — Won Area International Trial, East of England Show
  — 3rd King George V Gold Cup, Royal International Horse Show
September — 2nd A3 class, St. Gallen
October — Won Everest Double Glazing Championship
  — 2nd Radio Rentals Trophy, Horse of the Year Show
  — Equal 4th Leading Show Jumper of the Year, Horse of the
    Year Show

1976 Season (ridden by Paddy McMahon)
April — Won South Yorkshire Championship, Pageant of the Horse
May — Won Area International Trial, Shropshire and West Midland
June — Won Cockburn Stakes, Bath and West Show
  — 2nd Area International Trial, Three Counties Show
July — Won Texaco Championship, Royal Show
  — Won Area International Trial, Northampton
September — Won Raleigh Trophy, Burghley
October — 5th Sunday Times Cup, Horse of the Year Show
November — Won class, Amsterdam Show
  — 3rd Puissance, Brussels
December — 2nd class, Olympia Show

1977 Season (ridden by Geoff Glazzard)
May — 8th Open, Crane Hill *(first show ridden by Geoff Glazzard)*
  — Won the Jenkinsons Stakes, Staffordshire County
  — Won the Bass Worthington Competition, Staffordshire County
June — Won third leg Professional Championship, Cardiff
July — Won Area International Trial, Wales and West
  — Won Hennessy Trophy, Royal Show
  — 2nd Radio Rentals Championship, Royal Show
  — Winner of Leading Rider Award, Royal Show
  — Won Grand Prix, Billing Show
  — Equal 3rd King George V Gold Cup, Royal International Horse
    Show
  — Won Area International Trial, Northampton
August — 2nd class, Rotterdam Show
  — Won Area International Trial, British Timken

October – Equal 1st Butlins Championship, Horse of the Year Show
– 3rd Radio Rentals Stakes, Horse of the Year Show
December – 3rd Norwich Union Stakes, Olympia
– Equal 3rd Grand Prix, Olympia

1978 Season (ridden by Geoff Glazzard)

May – Won Grand Prix, Chippenham and Charlton Show
– 2nd Area International Trial, Shropshire & West Midland Show
June – Won Radio Rentals Stakes, Bath and West Show
– Won Area International Trial, Vauxhall Motors Show
– Won third leg Professional Championship, Cardiff
July – 3rd Everest Double Glazing Stakes, Royal Show
– 4th Radio Rentals B.S.J.A. National Championship, Royal Show
– Won Horse and Hound Cup, Royal International Horse Show
– Equal 4th King George V Gold Cup, Royal International Horse Show
August – Won Area International Trial, Anglesey
– Won class, Rotterdam
– 5th Grand Prix, Rotterdam
September – 2nd Area International Trial, Newbury Show
– Won Solaramic Championship, Everest Double Glazing Championships
December – 5th Harris Carpets Stakes, Olympia

GLOSSARY

Azoturia (Monday Morning Disease) — This disease is caused by enforced idleness of a horse in hard condition if the ration of corn is not reduced. The muscles of the loins become very hard and tense and stiffness sets in. **Page 56**

Docked — The practice of cutting off a portion of horse's tail. Under the Docking and Nicking Act, 1948, the practice is now illegal in Britain. **Page 47**

Hogged — The mane is completely shaved off by means of clippers. **Page 47**

F.E.I. — Fédération Equestre Internationale, the governing body of international equestrian sport. Founded in 1921 the headquarters are in Brussels. **Page 61**

h.h. — Hands High. A hand measures four inches. **Page 3**

Lunge — A means of training horses. They are fitted with a cavesson to which is attached a single rein; The horse can be circled to left and to right, made to walk, trot and canter and to halt and get used to and obey words of command. **Page 14**

Marl — Kind of rich soil often used as manure. **Page 71**

Nappiness — When a horse fails to respond to properly applied aids, refusing for example to go forward or to pass a certain point. **Page 16**

Puissance — A competition designed to test the horse's ability to jump height. **Page 4**

Rapping — The act of raising a pole, either at one end or at both ends, as a horse is jumping, so that the horse hits the pole and is thus encouraged to jump higher in future. Under F.E.I. and B.S.J.A. rules rapping is not permitted. **Page 50**

Roman Nose — A face with a convex, as opposed to the more usual concave, profile. **Page 3**

Surcingle — A webbing belt, usually 2½ to 3 inches wide, which is used to secure a rug. **Page 20**

INDEX

Erratum: Chapt. 1, Page 3, line 19
For 16 h.h. read 16·2 h.h.

144